AIRCRAFT ARCHIVE

A R C H I V E

CLASSICS OF WORLD WAR TWO

Argus Books
Wolsey House
Wolsey Road
Hemel Hempstead
Herts. HP2 4SS
England

First published by Argus Books 1989

ISBN 0 85242 985 1

Designed by Little Oak Studios
Phototypesetting by Typesetters (Birmingham) Ltd
Printed and bound in Great Britain by
William Clowes Limited, Beccles and London

Cover photo: Rebuilt by Personal Plane Services and
operated by Wessex Aviation and Transport of Henstridge,
the classic Westland Lysander flies again over Southern
England. (Peter March)

AIRCRAFT ARCHIVE

CLASSICS OF WORLD WAR TWO

Contents

A DETAILED COLLECTION OF ORIGINAL SCALE AIRCRAFT DRAWINGS

Introduction

In this, the seventh in our series of volumes on aircraft of World War II, we cover those types which do not necessarily fall neatly into the category of fighter or bomber, or which might otherwise be regarded as 'classics' of design or achievement. They include trainers, reconnaissance aircraft, communications aircraft, fleet spotters, a couple of noteworthy 'one-offs', and famous fighters which became national symbols characterised by shape and valiant battle records in the defence of their country.

Every aviation enthusiast has a personal favourite, and this selection of eighteen drawings must surely embrace more than a few of those first-loves. Many a pilot has good cause to express affection for the first primary trainer on which the treasured 'wings' were won. So we have the De Havilland 82A Tiger Moth, which provided the backbone of Elementary Flying Training Schools in the UK, the Union of South Africa, Rhodesia and Australia, and the Boeing-Stearman Kaydet which did such yeoman service in the Airschools of Canada and the USA. One stage on, and the Bücker Bü 133 Jungmeister is on record as the finest mount for solo aerobatics of its time, while for long and amazingly varied application the Polikarpov Po-2 must be included as the most adaptable workhorse ever to carry Soviet stars.

◄ The remarkable Fi 156 Storch was designed in 1935 and became a true workhorse of WWII. French-built Storchs are still flying, more than fifty years later. (IWM B7394)

For 'macho' shape, those monoplane fighters with open cockpits, the I-16 Rata and Macchi C200 Saetta, lend comparison with the heroic Polish PZL P-11c and the first (and last) of the German biplane fighters, the Heinkel He 51. Who can ignore those candidates for being slowest, the Storch and Lysander? Differing approaches to the same specification with similar achievement provide the aero-enthusiast with inspiration to model those daredevil tools of subterfuge.

One could go on – the elegant form of the Stösser, the last-ever biplane project in the Canadian Gregor and the encapsulated power of the Martin-Baker MB5 all demand study. But one aircraft stands above all, and for that reason, we allocate more space to the Focke-Wulf Fw 190. Drawn impeccably by Arthur Bentley to the most finite detail, this set of drawings represents the epitome of type-study and patient interpretation of remaining references as well as actual aircraft.

As we have mentioned in other volumes, every one of these drawings is a tribute to the skill and dedication of amateur researchers who produce something which very few of the manufacturers can provide! One such example is the Tiger Moth. Another which we dare claim as

◄ The preserved Macchi C200 on display at the Vigna di Valle Air Force Museum near Rome. Detailed plans of this famous fighter can be found on pages 60–64.

being more correct than any previous plan is that for the Polikarpov I-16, a drawing which we are publishing for the first time in these pages. BUT – knowing how fastidious many of our aeronautical 'nuts' are, we quite expect to be told that a line is a half millimetre or so out of place before the ink has a chance to dry! Another aspect with which we are specially pleased is that for the eighteen drawings we have sixteen different draughtsmen whose work has appeared over the years in the pages of *Aeromodeller* and *Scale Models*, and it is with universal gratitude, from ourselves as publishers and from the readers as consumers, that we acknowledge the contribution made by Arthur Bentley, Maurice Brett, Dennis Bryant, George Cox, Tony Datkiewicz, Geoff Duval, Bert Hatton, Björn Karlström, Pat Lloyd, Bill Nicholls, Felix Pawlowicz, Dave Platt, Giuliani Raimondi, Harry Robinson, Ian Stair and Harry Woodman to the annals of aviation history.

A *Jagdfliegerschule* prewar, showing Fw 56s (left), He 51s (right foreground) and Ar 65s in a mixture of *Luftwaffe* and civil markings; the Heinkel and Focke Wulf aircraft are featured in this volume.
▼

Polikarpov Po-2

Country of origin: USSR.
Type: Two-seat, land based training and general-purpose aircraft.
Dimensions: Wing span 37ft 4in *11.38m*; length 26ft 1in *7.95m*.

Weights: Empty 1918lb *870kg*.
Powerplant: One M-11 radial engine rated at 100hp.
Performance: Maximum speed 93mph *150kph*; service ceiling 12,530ft *3820m*;

range 250 miles *400km*.
Armament: None as trainer; various light ordnance when used in offensive roles.
Service: First flight 1927.

▲
Port elevation, Standard aircraft

◄ Scrap port elevation, Army version

Polish Po-2 (CSS-13) in Army service. Licence-built Polish machines featured tubular struts, revised control surfaces and undercarriage, and other modifications. (M Passingham)
▼

▲ Soviet Po-2 serving as a liaison and communications aircraft. The Po-2's flying surfaces were fabric covered, as were the sides and bottom of the fuselage. (M Passingham)

Scale

0 1 2 3 4 5 6 7 8 ft

0 1 2 m

A

D

B

▲ **Fuselage cross-sections**

SECTION E

Wing cross-section ▲
Upper and lower wing

TOP AND LOVER WING OF SIMILAR TWO-SPAR
ALL WOOD STRUCTURE. OPTIONAL AUXILIARY
PETROL TANK IN WING CENTER SECTION
19.5 GAL. CAPACITY.

PLYWOOD LEADING EDGE

FALSE SPAR

COMPRESSION RIB

FIXED
GUY WIRES

RED STAR

SPRUCE FRONT
SPAR

WING RIB

STAGGER 2.52'

E

RED NAV. LIGHT

YELLOW
OUTLINE

HAND HOLD

AILERON HORN

SPRUCE REAR SPAR

SPRUCE STRIP

WING
ATTACHMENT FITTING

AILERONS GAP WIRES
STREAMLINED SECTION

WING WALK REINFORCEMENT WITH
STEPS

1" WIDE PINKED
RIB TAPE

SIGHTING SLIT
(ARMY VERSION ONLY)
ON THE RIGHT
LOVER WING

WOODEN
FAIR-LEAD

ELEVATOR
HORN

▲ **Plan view, Standard aircraft**

METAL WHEEL
DISC

TURNBUCKLE

STREAMLINED
AXLE HOUSING

STRANDED STEEL
BRACING WIRES

TIRE VALVE ACCESS HOLE

▶ **Scrap view**
Undercarriage details

◄ Two members of the Soviet 46th 'Tamanskii' Guards Light Night Bomber Regiment, a unit whose personnel were exclusively female, pose in front of their Po-2s. (W Klepacki)

Ambulance version, showing method of transporting stretcher cases. Note external control wires running along fuselage. (M Passingham) ►

Scale

0 1 2 3 4 5 6 7 8 ft

0   1   2m

GREEN NAV. LIGHT

AIRSPEED STATIC TUBE

WIRES STAYS

LANDING LIGHT

ANCHOR RING

Port elevation, Ambulance version ▼

RED

RED WHITE

REMOVABLE TOP PART

SP-AEW

REMOVABLE TOP OF THE GONDOLA

FIXED BOTTOM PART

BLACK

WINDOW

FIXED PART OF THE GONDOLA

SNAP FASTENER

D   A   B

▲ **Front elevation, Standard aircraft**

Port elevation, S-13 ▼

FACTORY MARK /GREEN/

WSK POZNAŃ

TOWNEND RING (OPTIONAL)

WINDOW (BOTH SIDES)

VENTILATION HOLES

SLIDING WINDOW HATCH

FAIRING STRIPS

PLYWOOD BULKHEAD

PLYWOOD COVERING

BLACK

HANDLE

BLUE

A   B   C

▲ **Front elevation, Ambulance version**

LOTNICZA

SP-AXW

SILVER

WHITE

RED

SILVER LETTERING "LOTNICZE POGOTOWIE RATUNKOWE" (AIR-AMBULANCE SERVICE)

DRAWN BY F PAWLOWICZ

PO-2 AMBULANCE SP-AEW DURING FIRST YEARS AFTER II WORLD WAR WAS DONATED TO CIVIL AVIATION AND WAS IN THE SZCZECIN AEROCLUB IN POLAND

Plan view, Ambulance version ▶

Plan view, S-13 ▼

S·13

MODIFIED VERSION OF AIRCRAFT PO-2 WAS BUILT UNDER LICENCE IN POLAND AS CSS-13, THEY WERE BUILT IN AGRICULTURAL, TRAINER AND ARMY VERSIONS. THE AMBULANCE MODEL OF CSS-13, MARKED AS S-13 IS ILLUSTRATED.

RED
WHITE
BLACK OUTLINE
BLACK

RED
BLACK OUTLINE
WHITE

AILERON CONTROL CABLE
AILERON HINGE BRACKET
AILERON HORN

TAB CONTROL
ELEVATOR HINGE BRACKED
PLYWOOD LEADING EDGE
TRIM TAB (RED)

◀Fuselage cross-sections

BLUE ON THE BOTTOM WINGS AT FUSELAGE (UPPER SURFACES ONLY)

BLUE

Scrap views, S-13 ▼

SP-AXW

REGISTRATION : LOWER SURFACE – LEFT WING UPPER SURFACE – RIGHT WING

Polikarpov U-2 trainers, the furthest aircraft bearing a civil registration although a similar-style tail number to the other. (M Passingham)

Polish-built CSS-13 equipped with ski undercarriage. Note also landing light beneath port wing, and wing-tip skids. (M Passingham)

Scrap views, Standard aircraft
Ski undercarriage

Scrap view (not to scale)
Instrument panel (front cockpit), S-13/CSS-13

Scrap view, Standard aircraft
Cockpit details

Key to instrument panel
1. Throttle. 2. Electrical control. 3. Ignition switch. 4. Pneumatic fuel gauge. 5. Fuel gauge switch. 6. Airspeed indicator. 7. Altimeter. 8. Compass. 9. Turn and bank indicator. 10. Tachometer. 11. Engine primer. 12. Carburettor air thermometer. 13. Engine gauge. 14. Fuel tank (33.5gal capacity). 15. Control stick. 16. Rudder bar. 17. Rate of climb indicator. 18. Artificial horizon.

Key to cockpit details
1. Fuel tank. 2. Front instrument panel. 3. Pilot's control stick. 4. Throttle lever. 5. Wood bracket (port side). 6. Padded lining. 7. Rear instrument panel. 8. Seat. 9. Rear control stick (detachable). 10. Floorboard. 11. Mixture control lever. 12. Engine heater shut off. 13. Starting magneto (starboard side). 14. Control column thrust tube. 15. Rudder bar thrust tube. 16. Main rudder bar.

De Havilland DH82A Tiger Moth

Country of origin: Great Britain.
Type: Two-seat, land-based primary trainer.
Dimensions: Wing span 29ft 4in *8.94m*; length 23ft 11in *7.29m*; height 8ft 9½in *2.68m*; wing area 239 sq ft *22.2m²*.
Weights: Empty 1115lb *506kg*; maximum

1825lb *828kg*.
Powerplant: One De Havilland Gipsy Major four-cylinder, inverted, air-cooled engine rated at 130hp.
Performance: Maximum speed 109mph *175kph* at sea level; initial climb rate 673ft/min *196m/min*; service ceiling

13,600ft *4150m*.
Armament: None.
Service: First flight (DH60T) September 1931, (prototype Tiger Moth) 26 October 1931; service entry November 1931.

▲ Front elevation

▲ Starboard elevation

A Royal Navy Tiger Moth, photographed in 1947 at Eaton Bray. This aircraft was formerly G-ABRC, impressed into military service *circa* 1940.
▼

▲
G-ADUK of the London Aeroplane Club, being flown solo, 1948. Nearly 9000 Tiger Moths were built, many being released to civil flying clubs postwar at knock-down prices. (De Havilland)

Scrap view
Instrument panel
▼

Seat detail

Cable guide

▲
Port elevation

Tiger Moth II R5130 in wartime colours of Dark Earth and Dark Green camouflage, with yellow undersurfaces.
▼

Scale

0 1 2 3 4 5 6 7 8 ft
0 1 2m

Plan view ▼

Colour notes

G-ACDC: Fuselage, all struts, wing lettering – deep red. All flying surfaces and fuel tank – silver. Fuselage lettering – white. Wheel discs – silver.
G-ASKP: Overall finish – chrome yellow. Interplane struts, fuselage stripes, all lettering – mid-blue. Fuselage undersurfaces and undercarriage legs – black. Border of fuselage stripes – white.
General: Cockpit interior – dull green. Airscrew – grey. Airscrew tips – yellow.

S

S

Undersurface of slat position

Fabric strip along upper surface of elevator and aileron hinge

Black carborundum paint

15

A

◄ **Scrap underplan**
Tailplane

Centre Section Detail

D

5
6

14
15
16

Tank underside

C   B   A

◄ **Fuselage cross-sections**

2

No strokes on G-ACDC

7   13   12   1

▲
Scrap plan view
Fuselage, with wing omitted

One of the 3000 or so Tiger Moths built by Morris Motors during the war. Note the first aid access panel just aft of the roundel.
▼

NT·996

Aileron cables
51

Inspection patch

Trestle rest
52

▲ Scrap underplan

A flight of Tiger Moths, two in military markings, photographed prewar. During the desperate days of 1940, plans were laid to use the type as a fighter and a bomber should the need arise. (De Havilland) ▶

Scale

0 1 2 3 4 5 6 7 8 ft
0   1   2 m

Scrap view
Structure
▼

Scrap views ▲
Fin and rudder construction

Scrap port elevation
Interplane struts
▼

D

1½" dia disc

Tie down eye
at base of strut

8

F

E

Cockpit instrumentation is basic, as befits a primary trainer. The crash pads are prominent in this view, which also shows to advantage the non-slip wing walk area for the crew.
▼

E

▲
Scrap underplan
Upper port wing

Scrap underplan
Lower port wing
▼

F

G-ACDC

8

G-ASKP

Registration letters below port wing only on G-ASKP
None on upper surfaces

DRAWN BY D BRYANT

Numerical key

1. First aid stowage. 2. Chafing plates on anti-spin strakes. 3. Leather-covered crash pad. 4. Rear-view mirror. 5. Handgrips (front cockpit only). 6. Slot for safety harness. 7. Corrugated step plate. 8. Trailing edge slopes up from aileron to root. 9. Intercom and baggage stowage. 10. Fuel gauge. 11. Slots. 12. Magneto switches. 13. Oil tank (mounted externally for cooling). 14. Metal retaining plates. 15. Corrugations flattened locally to give smooth strip. 16. Flat cover plate over spar channel in tank. 17. Connector pipe across bridge of tank. 18. Fuel sump. 19. Fuel shut-off rod. 20. Drain cock. 21. Venturi (both sides). 22. Pressed aluminium fairing. 23. Overflow pipe fairing. 24. Steadying arm for aileron return cable. 25. Filler cap. 26. Overflow valve. 27. Skid detail. 28. Carburettor air intake. 29. Aileron cam detail. 30. Leather cuff. 31. Map pocket. 32. Spring bias on rudder. 33. Slot locking lever. 34. Slot locking handgrips. 35. Parallel-action rudder pedals. 36. Front seat mounted in diagonal bulkhead. 37. Jacking pad. 38. Rudder linking rod. 39. Spring bias for tail trimming. 40. Door catches. 41. Tail trim connecting rod. 42. Throttle. 43. Air speed indicator. 44. Deviation card holder. 45. Altimeter. 46. Crash pad. 47. Turn and bank indicator. 48. Engine speed indicator. 49. Oil pressure indicator (red). 50. Pull tab for first aid access. 51. ¾in × ½in wood strips. 52. Pitot tubes.

Sketch section

PZL P11c

Country of origin: Poland.
Type: Single-seat, land-based interceptor fighter and fighter-bomber.
Dimensions: Wing span 35ft 2in *10.79m*; length 24ft 9½in *7.56m*; height 9ft 4in *2.84m*; wing area 192.7 sq ft *17.9m²*.
Weights: Empty 2443lb *1108kg*; loaded 3505lb *1590kg*.
Powerplant: One Bristol Mercury VI S2 nine-cylinder radial engine rated at 645hp.
Performance: Maximum speed 242mph *390kph* at 18,050ft *5500m*; time to 16,400ft *5000m*, 6min; service ceiling 36,100ft *11,000m*; range 503 miles *810km*.
Armament: Two or four fixed 7.7mm KM Wz33 machine guns, plus two 27lb *12.25kg* bombs.
Service: First flight (P11/I prototype) October 1931; service entry (P11a) 1934, (P11c) late 1934.

▲ **Port elevation**

Colour notes
Olive green overall except lower surfaces of wings and tailplane which were light blue-grey.

No 113 Squadron Polish Air Force P11cs at Okecie Airport, Warsaw; the fourth machine in line is in fact a P6, as noted on the fin tip. Emergency production of the P11 was halted by the German invasion, and only some 250 were built. (M Passingham)
▼

Numerical key

1. Mirror. 2. Fuel tank. 3. Hand grip. 4. Compass. 5. Boost. 6. Fuel pressure. 7. Emergency fuel cut-off. 8. Oil temperature (out). 9. Brake drum and cable. 10. Jacking point. 11. Fuel gauge. 12. Oil temperature (in). 13. Oil pressure. 14. Air speed indicator/artificial horizon. 15. Compass deviation table. 16. Bank indicator. 17. Engine rpm. 18. Altimeter. 19. Rate of fuel flow control. 20. Clock. 21. Bomb release control. 22. Harness tension control. 23. Boost control. 24. Throttle. 25. Radio. 26. Fuselage guns trigger button. 27. Wing guns trigger button. 28. Oil tank. 29. Fuel header tank. 30. Rudder pedals. 31. Brake control. 32. Ammunition box. 33. Dual-purpose ailerons/flaps. 34. Signal cartridges rack. 35. Gun mountings. 36. Elevator trim. 37. Very pistol. 38. Pilot's locker. 39. First aid. 40. Gun servicing hatch. 41. Air intake control. 42. Seat adjustment. 43. Opening for Very pistol. 44. Elevator trim gear. 45. Foot rests. 46. Fuel inlet. 47. Bomb rack (12.5kg). 48. Air speed indicator pitot. 49. Venturi. 50. Oil cooler. 51. Exhaust. 52. Exhaust collector. 53. Corrugated duralumin (8 corrugations per inch). 54. Rubber covering (to prevent shell damage by cases and links). 55. Tan leather. 56. Detachable panel over oil tank. 57. KM Wz33 guns. 58. Camera.

▲
The PZL P6 prototype. This and the P7 were the direct progenitors of the P11, the inline-engined P8/9/10 series being discarded in favour of the radial-engined 7 and 11. (M Passingham)

▲
Scrap starboard elevation

Scrap views
Cockpit details
▼

Scale

0 1 2 3 4 5 6 7 8ft
0   1   2m

◀ **Plan view**

▲
Wing cross-sections

DRAWN BY Z A DATKIEWICZ

▲ A captured P11c is manhandled away. Note the faded national insignia on the upper wing and the 113 ('Owl') Squadron marking on the fuselage. (M Passingham)

WHITE NUMERALS

Front elevation ▼

DURAL
8 CORRUGATIONS = INCH

BLACK RUBBER

Fuselage cross-sections ▼

▲ Underplan

Heinkel He 51B-1

Country of origin: Germany.
Type: Single-seat, land-based fighter.
Dimensions: Wing span 36ft 1in *11.00m*; length 27ft 6¾in *8.40m*; height 10ft 6in *3.20m*; wing area 292.78 sq ft *27.2m²*.
Weights: Empty 3247lb *1472kg*; normal loaded 4189lb *1900kg*.

Powerplant: One BMW VI 7.3Z twelve-cylinder, liquid-cooled engine rated at 750hp.
Performance: Maximum speed 205mph *330kph* at sea level; time to 3280ft *1000m*, 1.4min; service ceiling 25,260ft *7700m*; range 354 miles *570km*.

Armament: Two fixed 7.9mm MG 17 machine guns.
Service: First flight (He 51a) summer 1933, (He 51A-0) July 1934, (A-1) April 1935; service entry (B-1) early 1936.

Port elevation ▲

◀ Scrap starboard elevation

Scale
0 1 2 3 4 5 6 7 8 ft
0   1   2m

He 51A, probably the first A-0 pre-production aircraft D-IQEE. Differences between the A and B versions were minimal. (M Passingham) ▼

DRAWN BY C J NICHOLLS

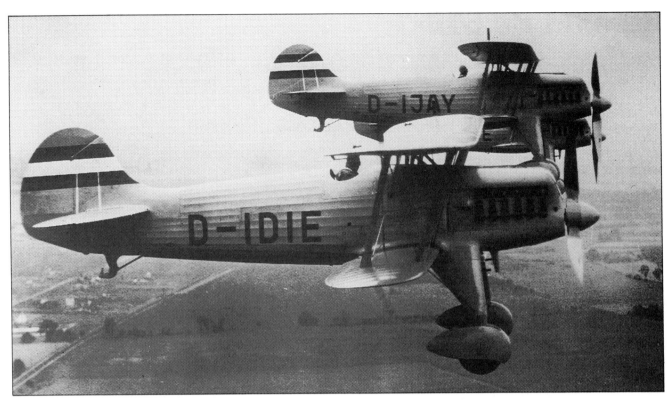

A 1934 photograph showing three pre-production He 51s; A-05 (nearest camera) and A-04 can be identified. (Pilot Press)

Notes

He 51A-1: Single undercarriage bracing; cuffed propeller.

He 51B-1: Double undercarriage bracing; external fuel tank. All types sometimes discarded spats.

Plan view ▲

Compass fairing.

Gunsight.

Mirror.

Fuselage cross-sections ▼

◄ Front elevation

Pitot.

Radiator flap fully open.

Lower Wing Section 'P'

L/W Section 'R'

L/W Section 'S'

Underplan
▼

Strut Section 'W'

Strut Section 'X'

Strut cross-sections ▲

Upp. Wing ℄ Section

U/W Section 'L'

U/W Section 'M'

U/W Section 'N'

▲
Wing cross-sections

Tailplane cross-sections
▼

Section 'T'

Section 'V'

E

Cockpit door.

K

An He 51B of *2 Staffel, I Gruppe*. The He 51 served during WWII, but generally in a training capacity. (H Woodman)
▼

Focke-Wulf Fw 56 Stösser (Falcon)

Country of origin: Germany.
Type: Single-seat, land-based advanced trainer.
Dimensions: Wing span 34ft 7½in *10.55m*; length 25ft 1in *7.65m*; height 8ft 4½in *2.55m*; wing area 150.7 sq ft *14.0m²*.
Weights: Empty 1477lb *670kg*; loaded

2172lb *985kg*.
Powerplant: One Argus As 10C eight-cylinder, inverted-vee, air-cooled engine rated at 240hp.
Performance: Maximum speed 173mph *278kph* at sea level; time to 3280ft *1000m*, 2.2min; service ceiling 20,340ft

6200m*; range 239 miles *385km*.
Armament: One or two fixed 7.92mm MG 17 machine guns, plus up to three 22lb *10kg* bombs.
Service: First flight (Fw 56 V1) November 1933; service entry 1937.

◄ Port elevation

Scrap view
Structure
▼

Fuselage cross-sections
▼

Head-on shot of D-IIZE shows the elegant streamlining of the Fw 56 parasol fighter-trainer. The asymmetric exhaust pipes are well in evidence here.
▼

The celebrated aerobatic pilot Gerd Achgelis poses in his non-standard Stösser demonstrator D-IKNI (270hp Argus) at Los Angeles before the war. ►

◄ Underplan

On D-IKNI only
Opening for oil cooler on D-IKNI only
Hinge.

Not on D-IKNI

▲ Wing cross-section (approx)

P.s. only.
JURY STRUT

Inspection panels hinged forward

Scrap underplan ▲
True view of wing strut, starboard side

Windows on D-IKNI only
Gun sight not on D-IKNI

Bulge over m.g. belt feed (not on D-IKNI)
Holes for c.s. bracing wires

Tube fairing over m.g.
Hinges

Panel on D-IKNI & early production aircraft

▲ **Scrap views**
Cowling details

Scale

0 1 2 3 4 5 6 7 8 ft
0   1   2 m

◀ Fw 56 cockpit, showing 'spade' type grip on control column and Revi gun sight offset to the right on top of cowl.

Plan view
▼

Machine gun sight lettering
Hell = light, Dunkel = dark.

Key to cockpit layout
1. Switch. 2. Clock. 3. Altimeter. 4. Air speed indicator. 5. Compass (with magnet adjustments top and bottom). 6. Turn indicator. 7. Electric machine gun sight plug. 8. Compass deviation card. 9. Engine rpm. 10. Carburettor heat switch. 11. Manifold pressure. 12. Oil pressure. 13. Oil temperature. 14. Dive brake. 15. Elevator trim. 16. Rudder trim. 17. Fuel cut-off. 18. Fuel reserve switches. 19. Generator on/off. 20. Map case. 21. Aircraft service card. 22. Hand pump.

Plywood deck under fabric
Hinged access doors to cockpit
Hand holds hinged forward

Painted marks on top surface only

Painted marks on top surface only

DRAWN BY IAN R STAIR

◀ Forward fuselage top panelling removed to reveal pristine engine and mountings, with starboard machine gun installed above. Note Argus logo on forward crankcase.

◀ Starboard elevation

Ammo box door
not on D-IKNI

Window on D-IKNI only

FOCKE-WULF
"STÖSSER"

Hinge to fabric covered
inspection panel
Fuel drain
Fuel sump
Wheel pant mount on D-IKNI
(pants not used)

On D-IKNI only
Not on D-IKNI
Wheel covers glossy black

Scale

0 1 2 3 4 5 6 7 8 ft

0   1   2 m

Wheels in flying position

Heine propeller.
Mahogany with
brass edge strips

Not on D-IKNI
D-IKNI only

Rolled interlocking
edges to u/c fairing

▲
Front elevation

**Peacetime aerobatic shot shows well
the Fw 56's wing planform, with
tailplane set well forward from the fin.**
▼

Polikarpov I-16

Country of origin: USSR.
Type: Single-seat, land-based fighter and fighter-bomber.
Dimensions: Wing span 29ft 6½in *9.00m*; length 20ft 1¼in *6.13m*; height 8ft 5in *2.57m*; wing area 161 sq ft *14.96m²*.
Weights: Empty 3285lb *1490kg*; normal

loaded 4212lb *1910kg*; maximum 4547lb *2062kg*.
Powerplant: One Shvetsov M-62 nine-cylinder radial engine rated at 1000hp.
Performance: Maximum speed 326mph *525kph* at sea level; service ceiling 29,500ft *9000m*; range (max external

fuel) 435 miles *700km*.
Armament: Two fixed 20mm ShVAK cannon and two fixed 7.62mm ShKAS machine guns, plus six 82mm RS82 rockets or equivalent load.
Service: First flight (prototype) December 1933; service entry late 1934.

DRAWN BY A A P LLOYD

Gunsight.
Radio access.
U/C Retract wire.
Canopy slides forward along gunsight barrel for access.

▲ Starboard elevation, Type 5

MARKINGS FOR
Nº 13 "Za USSR".

White.
ЗА СССР! ☆ Red.
13

Scale
0 1 2 3 4 5 6 7 8 ft
0 1 2 m

I-16s fought in the Spanish Civil War on both sides; this Type 6, powered by a 730hp M-25A, was one of a number supplied to the Republican Air Force. Note cockpit canopy slid into the aft position.
▼

" Za STALINA " Nº 11.
White.
Dark Green.
Red.
White.
За СТАЛИНА ☆
Colour division line.
Pale Blue.

▲ Port elevation, Type 24

▲
Type 6 in Nationalist markings, one of eighteen captured from the Republicans. Canopy is slid forward in this view.

Fuselage cross-sections, Type 5
▼

This side of centreline shows wing construction details. Undersurface details are not projected through. (K)

Pitot.

7·62mm Machine gun.

(J)

(I)

(L)

N.B. Fin offset.

◄ **Plan view, Type 5**

▲
Fuselage cross-sections, Type 24

Wing and tailplane cross-sections ▶

▲Underplan, Type 5

Construction details
shown above centre-
line. Uppersurface
details not projected
through.

▲
Scrap front elevation, Type 24

Front elevation, Type 5 ▶

Brake cable.

Lowest segment of door is pushed
upward and outward by lever and link.

Undercarriage
retracting wires.

Scale

0 1 2 3 4 5 6 7 8 ft

0   1   2 m

Advanced in concept when first introduced, the Soviet Air Force's I-16s were obsolete by 1941 but they nevertheless bore the brunt of the early *Luftwaffe* offensive during 'Barbarossa'. ▶

Scrap view (not to scale) ▶
Instrument panel

Typical ski installation, fixed position.

▲
Port elevation, Type 5

▲
Scrap plan view, Type 24

◀ I-16s were in service with the Spanish Air Force well into the 1950s and this photograph shows C.8-25, believed to be the last example on strength.

A poor-quality photo of a Soviet I-16 that has come to grief gives an idea of the slotted engine cowling and domed spinner. ▶

Bücker Bü 133 Jungmeister

Country of origin: Germany.
Type: Single-seat, land-based advanced trainer.
Dimensions: Wing span 21ft 7½in *6.60m*; length 19ft 4in *5.90m*; height 7ft 4½in *2.25m*; wing area 129 sq ft *12.0m²*.

Weights: Empty 926lb *420kg*; loaded 1292lb *586kg*.
Powerplant: One Siemens Sh 14A-4 seven-cylinder radial engine rated at 160hp.
Performance: Maximum speed 134mph

216kph; initial climb rate 1170ft/min *355m/min*; service ceiling 20,000ft *6100m*; range 310 miles *500km*.
Armament: None.
Service: First flight 1935.

Scale
0 1 2 3 4 5 6 7 8ft
0   1   2m

Port elevation, Prototype ▶
Sh 14A-4 engine

SILVER
OVERALL

▲
Starboard elevation, Prototype
Hirth HM 506 engine

DRAWN BY G A G COX

A classic by any standards, the Jungmeister is still a favoured aerobatic aircraft. This one sports a Swiss registration.
▼

▲
Another Swiss-registered Bü 133, built by Dornier in 1940 and one of the subjects of our drawings.

Front elevation ▶
Sh 14A-4 engine

Port elevation ▲
Sh 14A-4 engine

◀ **Fuselage cross-sections**

Numerical key
1. This strut port side only. 2. Black wing walk port side, all aircraft. 3. Zip fastener on inspection flap. 4. Mudguards often discarded. 5. Fabric lacing all along underside. 6. Petrol tank. 7. Metal panels. 8. Undercarriage in offload position. 9. No framing to this windshield. 10. Fuel gauge. 11. Colour lines. 12. Leather cuffs round interplane strut ends and tailwheel leg. 13. Leather crashpad. 14. Venturi tube. 15. Altimeter. 16. Clock. 17. Oil temperature. 18. Air speed indicator. 19. Accelerometer. 20. Engine rpm. 21. Oil pressure. 22. Fuel pressure. 23. Priming pump. 24. Toe brake pedal.

◄ **Plan view**
*Starboard side,
Sh 14A-4 engine*

Plan view
*Port side, Super
Scarab engine* ▼

▲ **Scrap front elevation**
Hirth HM 506 engine

REGISTRATION
WITH WHITE
BACKGROUND
HERE ON
STARBOARD
UPPER WING

◄ **Underplan**
*Starboard side,
Sh 14A-4 engine*

BEVERLY HOWARD'S
JUNGMEISTER WITH
WARNER SUPER SCARAB
ENGINE

▲ **Starboard elevation**
Super Scarab engine

▲ **Underplan**
Port side, Super Scarab engine

Scale

```
0  1  2  3  4  5  6  7  8 ft
0         1         2 m
```

HB-MIC in yellow paintwork, with red
trim and cowling blisters,
photographed in 1958. The Jungmeister
was an important element in the
prewar *Luftwaffe* training programme.
▼

▲
Count Cantacuzene's Jungmeister, well-known participant at aerobatic contests in the 1950s. Note rudder extension.

Sketch section

Bü 133 instrument panel, considerably different from that depicted in the accompanying sketch and reflecting the 'customised' nature of privately owned Jungmeisters postwar.
▼

Curtiss SBC-3 and -4 Helldiver

Country of origin: USA.
Type: Two-seat, carrier-based scout bomber.
Dimensions: Wing span 34ft 0in *10.36m*; length 27ft 5in *8.36m*; height 10ft 3½in *3.14m*; wing area 317 sq ft *29.45m²*.
Weights: Empty 4166lb *1889kg*, (-4) 4841lb *2195kg*; loaded 5581lb *2531kg*, (-4) 7632lb *3461kg*.

Powerplant: One Pratt & Whitney R-1535-94 Twin Wasp radial engine rated at 825hp, (-4) Wright R-1820-34 Cyclone rated at 950hp.
Performance: (-4) Maximum speed 235mph *378kph*; initial climb rate 1450ft/min *440m/min*; service ceiling 24,500ft *7470m*; range 610 miles *982km*.
Armament: One fixed 0.3in or 0.5in Colt

machine gun and one flexibly mounted 0.3in machine gun, plus one 500lb *227kg* or (-4) 1000lb *454kg* bomb beneath fuselage and one 100lb *45kg* bomb under each wing.
Service: First flight (XSBC-1) January 1934, (XSBC-3) March 1936; service entry (SBC-3) July 1937, (-4) 1938.

▲ Port elevation, SBC-3

Colour notes

SBC-3: Tail surfaces, excluding fillets – red. Top surface of upper wing – chrome yellow. All other metal surfaces – light grey. Lower wings – silver. Engine cowling, wing chevron and fuselage band – blue with white border. VS-5 badge – black man o' war bird with red throat; red border to white diamond. White 'S', hyphens and tail lettering.
XSBC-4: Serial 0582. From station 'B' aft – as

SBC-4 except where indicated. Colour – all polished metal and silver dope, all lettering black.
SBC-4: Basic fuselage and wing colours as SBC-3. Tail, including fillets – blue (USS *Enterprise*). Cowl and fuselage bands – blue with white outline. Lettering – black (except white on tail). Carrier emblem – white disc with blue ship and surrounding circle.

The SBC was the last front-line military biplane to be produced in the USA, and was in service when war broke out in the Pacific. This is an SBC-4, powered by a 950hp Wright Cyclone.
▼

Close-in air-to-air view of an SBC-4, showing to advantage the streamlined centre-section strut fairings and retracted port main wheel. The immense width of the aircraft's ailerons is also apparent. ▶

▲
Scrap front elevation, SBC-3
Twin Wasp installation

Lettering this
size on XSBC-4

U/C door fills
this space XSBC-4

Two extra
gills XSBC-4

Blue band

Off-load position
SBC-3 similar, but
with 6" solid wheel

▲
Starboard elevation, SBC-4

A number of SBC-4s on order for France were diverted to the RAF, where they were dubbed Clevelands. This one has a ground instructional serial number.
▼

Scale

Fuselage cross-sections
▼

A B

C

F G

D E

H J

K L

◄ Plan view, SBC-4
Starboard side

Extra gill left side

▲
Scrap plan view/
underplan, SBC-3

DRAWN BY G A G COX

◄ Underplan, SBC-4
Starboard side

Scale
0 1 2 3 4 5 6 7 8 ft
0   1   2 m

SBC-4 registered as NX-C5 in French camouflage and
markings. The underbelly fuel tank held 41.5 gallons. Note
open cowl flap.
▼

Fieseler Fi 156C Storch

Country of origin: Germany.
Type: Three-seat, land-based communications, army co-operation and general-purpose aircraft.
Dimensions: Wing span 46ft 9in *14.25m*; length 32ft 6in *9.91m*; height 10ft 0in *3.05m*; wing area 279.9 sq ft *26.0m²*.

Weights: Empty 2051lb *930kg*; loaded 2924lb *1326kg*.
Powerplant: One Argus As 10C eight-cylinder, inverted-vee, air-cooled engine rated at 240hp.
Performance: Maximum speed 109mph *175kph* at sea level; time to 3000ft *915m*,

4min; service ceiling 16,700ft *5090m*; range 630 miles *1015km*.
Armament: One flexibly mounted 7.9mm MG 15 machine gun.
Service: First flight (V1) spring 1936; service entry (C-1) early 1939, (C-3) late 1940.

▲ Port elevation

Scrap starboard elevation ▼

▲ Fuselage cross-sections

Able to take off and land in incredibly short distances, the Storch (Stork) was the standard German army co-operation and light observation aircraft of the war. This depicts an early C-1, camouflaged yet bearing a civil registration. (L Whitehouse) ▼

▲Plan view

ANGULAR TAIL LINES OF
MORANE BUILT STORCH.

FABRIC
COVERING

PLYWOOD
COVERING

PLYWOOD COVERING

FABRIC COVERING

WHITE ONLY

FARBTON 7I (BS. 5·06I)
FOREST GREEN (LEYLAC
COLOURS) UPPER SURFACE.

The huge area of glazing gave the crew a superb view out
of the cockpit – even downwards!
▼

Damaged *Luftwaffe* Fi 156 ambulance of a
Wüstennotstaffel (Desert Rescue Squadron); note
additional triangular glazing of this D model. (L Whitehouse)
▼

▲
Storchs were produced in France as the MS.500 'Criquet' series; here an MS.502 fuselage awaits restoration work.

▲
Front cockpit detail of a WWII *Luftwaffe* Storch, showing compact instrument panel.

INVERTED SLAT NOT FITTED TO LATER VERSIONS

LACING

Scrap underplan ▶

TRIM

FLAPS

BLUISH WHITE UNDER SIDES

LACING

SLATS (FIXED)

2.33°

MASS BALANCE

LANDING LIGHT (PORT WING)

PITOT (PORT WING)

STEP

EXHAUST

OIL COOLER

Scale

0 1 2 3 4 5 6 7 8 ft

0   1   2 m

▲
Fi 156C D-INBC again, here with wings folded back. Entire leading edge of wing was occupied by slots. (L Whitehouse)

Front elevation
▼

FUEL GAUGE

LANDING LIGHT

MAX. COMPRESSED

SHOCK TRAVEL →

BRAKE LINE

STEP

FLIGHT POSITION

DRAWN BY BJÖRN KARLSTRÖM

◄ VD+TD was one of several Storchs captured by the British and is seen here in the UK daubed as Air Ministry No 99. (IWM B6199)

Boeing-Stearman PT-13–18 Kaydet

Country of origin: USA.
Type: Two-seat, land-based primary trainer.
Dimensions: Wing span 32ft 2in *9.80m*; length 25ft 0¼in *7.63m*; height 9ft 2in *2.79m*; wing area 297.4 sq ft *27.63m²*.

Weights: Empty 1936lb *878kg*; loaded 2717lb *1232kg*.
Powerplant: One Lycoming R-680 radial engine rated at 220hp, (PT-17) Continental R-670 rated at 220hp, (PT-18) Jacobs R-755 rated at 225hp.

Performance: Maximum speed 124mph *200kph*; initial climb rate 840ft/min *256m/min*; service ceiling 11,200ft *3400m*; range 505 miles *813km*.
Armament: None.
Service: First flight: (PT-13) 1936.

▲ Port elevation

Fuselage cross-sections ▼

PT 13 D

MCCAULEY STEEL PROPELLER

▲ Wing and tailplane cross-sections

US Army PT-13D, its Lycoming R-680-17 engine distinguished by the frontal exhaust collector ring. Colours are chrome yellow flying surfaces and blue fuselage. (R Stouffer) ▼

DRAWN BY G A G COX

Plan view
Starboard side
▼

Underplan
Starboard side
▼

PT 13D

COLOUR PT 13 D
BRIGHT BLUE - FUSELAGE
ALL STRUTS
SPACER 'S'
CHROME YELLOW - WINGS
TAIL
RIGGING WIRES
NUMERALS ON FUSELAGE
ALUMINIUM   WHEEL DISCS

LOCATION OF LETTERING
(SOLID BLACK)

COLOUR - N 2S·5
ALL YELLOW

BLACK (BOTH SERVICES) WING WALKS, HANDLES,
COCKPIT EDGE PADDING & TAILWHEEL CUFF.

SENSENICH WOODEN PROPELLER

▲
A Stearman N2S-3 in Navy markings. This model was the same as the N2S-1, except for the fitting of a later-model Continental R-670-4 engine. (R Stouffer)

US Navy N2S-4, with Continental engine, seen at the 1984 Annual Stearman Convention and fly-in, Galesburg, Illinois. (R Stouffer)
▼

Sketch section

Numerical key
1. Firewall. 2. Baggage compartment. 3. Instrument panels. 4. Fire extinguisher. 5. Throttle. 6. Control lock lever. 7. Rudder pedal. 8. Elevator trim. 9. Corrugated heel boards. 10. Link rod to aileron crank. 11. Aileron crank. 12. Step. 13. Petrol filler cap. 14. Oil filler cap. 15. Static discharge rod. 16. Carburettor air intake. 17. Magneto switch operating rod. 18. Fuel gauge. 19. Elevator control tube. 20. Engine rpm. 21. Oil temperature and pressure. 22. Clock. 23. ASI. 24. Compass. 25. Altimeter. 26. Instrument panel, bevelled along sight lines. 27. Inertia starting handle (rear cockpit only). 28. Rudder cable. 29. Magneto switch. 30. Fuel cock. 31. Front seat. 32. Mounting lugs for pedals. 33. Complete undercarriage assembly detaches. 34. Engine mounting lugs. 35. Cowling attachment points. 36. Canvas cover. 37. Front spar mounting.

▲
PT-13 in US Army decor. The Boeing-Stearman was the longest serving biplane trainer, and many still fly today for sport or as crop-dusters. (M Passingham)

PT 13 D NUMERALS

Scrap underplan
Upper wing centre-section

Scrap views ▲ ▶
Showing internal structure

Colour notes, PT-13D
Fuselage, all struts, spacers – bright blue. Wings, tail, rigging wires, numerals on fuselage – chrome yellow. Wheel discs – aluminium. Wing walks, wing lettering, handles, cockpit edge padding, tailwheel cuff – black.

Front elevation ▲

LYCOMING
R·680·17

Fairey Seafox

Country of origin: Great Britain.
Type: Two-seat, ship-based light reconnaissance seaplane.
Dimensions: Wing span 40ft 0in *12.19m*; length 33ft 5½in *10.20m*; height 12ft 2in *3.71m*; wing area 434 sq ft *40.32m²*.
Weights: Empty 3805lb *1726kg*; loaded 5420lb *2458kg*; max catapulting 5650lb *2562kg*.
Powerplant: One Napier Rapier VI sixteen-cylinder, H type, air-cooled engine rated at 395hp.
Performance: Maximum speed 124mph *199.6kph*; initial climb rate 420ft/min *130m/min*; service ceiling 9700ft *2950m*; range 440 miles *710km*.
Armament: One flexibly mounted 0.303in Lewis machine gun.
Service: First flight (prototype) 27 May 1936; service entry 23 April 1937.

◄ Port elevation

Scale

Port inboard profile ►

INSTRUMENT PANEL
ENGINE CONTROL LEVERS (PORT)
AMMUNITION DRUMS (STBD)
FAIREY GUN MOUNTING
GUN SPARES (STBD)
RADIO EQUIPMENT
WIRELESS AERIAL
OBSERVERS PARACHUTE (STBD)
ADJUSTABLE SEAT SUPPORT
CONTROL COLUMN
FLAP CONTROL WHEEL (PORT)
RUDDER PEDALS
CROSS SECTION OF SEAM

K8575, the seventh production Seafox, in its prewar aluminium finish. Flaps are lowered and rudder deflected to starboard. (H Woodman)
▼

CENTRE SECTION
LAMP FITTING

▲ Front elevation

SPIGOT. CHECKS WINGS
WHEN FOLDED.

BOMBS
ARRANGEMENT 'A' = 2 x 100lb.
ANTI-SUBMARINE BOMBS.
ARRANGEMENT 'B' = 8 x 20lb.
BOMBS.

UNIVERSAL No. I
CARRIER.

100lb. BOMB (H.E)
BODY YELLOW
NOSE BAND RED
SECOND BAND GREEN

STAY TUBES

LIGHT SERIES
BOMB CARRIER

R.A.F. 10 LB. PRACTICE BOMB
RED BAND AROUND NOSE
TWO BLUE BANDS AROUND BODY

MARINE MARKER
DARK GREEN

▲ Scrap views
Bomb carriage

▲ Propeller

ELEVATING QUADRANT

TRAVERSING QUADRANT

FROM ORIGINAL WORKS DRAWING

◄▲ Scrap views (not to scale)
Fairey gun mounting

Float struts and fitting ▼
Key
A. Front spar lug to pick up with locking bar
on wing root. B. Oil tank. C. Locking lug and
trestle point. D. Rubber buffer rings
between flanges on sliding leg and outer
casing. E. Water rudder control pulleys. F.
Sliding leg attached to lower part of strut
(lug) and end-of-travel buffer. G. Lid to
anchor stowage.

ALL OVER SILVER

ALL LETTERS
AND NUMBERS
BLACK.

K
8587

H9A

RED WARNING
STRIPS

▲ Scrap port elevations
Seafox of HMS Arethusa,
Mediterranean, June 1939

Fuselage cross-sections

A   B   C

Scrap view (not to scale)
Instrument layout

Plan view

DETACHABLE WING TIPS

NOTE: RUDDER & VERTICAL FIN
ASYMMETRIC IN PLAN VIEW

FULL FLOAT
SHOWING
PATTERN
OF FOOT
HOLDS.

X   Y

Float cross-sections

Scrap plan view
Float

Scale

0 1 2 3 4 5 6 7 8 ft

0   1   2 m

**Constructional photo showing engine
bearers, lower wing root detail (port
wing folded back) and float struts.** ▶

▲
The second prototype Seafox photographed on its
beaching gear during testing at Felixstowe. Note the
stylistic variations in the presentation of the serial numbers
on fuselage and fin. (H Woodman)

DRAWN BY HARRY WOODMAN

▲
Scrap plan view
Lower starboard wing

◄ Scrap underplan

POSITION OF WINGS
WHEN COMPLETELY FOLDED

Lower starboard wing prior to covering, showing metal-
sheathed leading edge and flap and aileron hinge lines.
▼

Westland Lysander Mks I, II and IIIA

Country of origin: Great Britain.
Type: Two-seat, land-based army co-operation and general-purpose aircraft.
Dimensions: Wing span 50ft 0in *15.24m*; length 30ft 6in *9.30m*; height 14ft 6in *4.42m*; wing area 260 sq ft *24.15m²*.
Weights: Empty 4365lb *1980kg*; loaded

6318lb *2865kg*.
Powerplant: One Bristol Mercury XII nine-cylinder radial engine rated at 890hp, (Mk II) Perseus XII rated at 905hp, (Mk III) Mercury XX or XXX rated at 870hp, (Mk IIIA) Mercury XXX rated at 870hp.
Performance: Maximum speed 212mph *341kph* at 5000ft *1525m*; initial climb rate

1410ft/min *430m/min*; service ceiling 21,500ft *6550m*.
Armament: Two fixed 0.303in Browning machine guns and one flexibly mounted Vickers K gun, plus up to six light bombs.
Service: First flight (prototype) 15 June 1936; service entry (Mk I) late 1938.

▲
Port elevation, Mk I
No 16 Squadron RAF, 1939

◄ **Scrap port elevation, Mk IIIA**
Gunner's cockpit

Scrap views
Undercarriage spats
▼

Prewar shot of a trio of Lysanders peeling off for the camera, the shape of the tailplanes identifying the machines as Mk IIs. The camouflage patterns of the two nearest aircraft are 'mirror images' of each other.
▼

▲
Propeller details

◄ Lysander II with wheel spat panels removed. A second aircraft is flying behind the subject of the photo, its starboard wheel just discernible. Finish is standard Dark Green and Dark Earth camouflage.

Port elevation, Mk IIIA
Special Air Service
▼

* INDICATES P
SLAT G

N.B.
KJ-O HAD
WING ROUND
LATE 1939

Scale
0 1 2 3 4 5 6 7 8 ft
0   1   2 m

NOSE OF MARK II.

PORT &
ST'BO.

PORT ONLY.

NM

22

RBL
W
RR

V9738

RR Y RBL W

TAILPLANE POSITION
FOR SLOW FLYING.
(FLAPS DOWN;
SLATS OPEN.)

SI

SPAT GUNS
DELETED.

LONG RANGE FUEL TANK.
('150 GALLONS.)

COLOUR - OVERALL SEMI-MATT BLACK.
UPPER WING ROUNDELS AS MK.I.
SERIAL NUMBERS : DULL RED.

DRAWN BY G R DUVAL

Scrap starboard elevation, Mk II ►

DE

DE
DE
DE

6   5   4   3   2   C   1

KJ-O

DE

DE

DE

8

7   19

FOUR ANTI-PERSONNEL
BOMBS; -(DG. WITH
WHITE BAND.)

MESSAGE PICK-UP HOOK - NM
(OMITTED FROM PORT SIDE VIEW
FOR CLARITY.)

DG   19

BRO

303" BROWNING
MACHINE GUN
IN SPAT.

INBOARD VIEW - STARBOARD SPAT.

DG

DE

S1 S2 S3 S4

S1   S2   S3   S4

▲ **Starboard elevation, Mk I**

COCKPIT FRONT
FRAME.

C   1   2   3   4   5   6 7   8

BALLAST
WEIGHTS.

E

ST'BO.
SIDE
ONLY.

MARK III
PANEL SHOWN.

LADDER, MK III S.A.S.

OUTBOARD SLAT HAS
INDEPENDENT ACTION.

W1   W3   W4

W2
SLAT CLOSED, FLAPS UP.

LINKED ACTION.

FLAP   W2   INBOARD
SLAT

▲ **Fuselage cross-sections**   **Wing cross-sections ►**

Scrap plan view
Stub wing detail ▲

SUPPLY CONTAINER RACK.

19

FUSELAGE C/L.

STUB WING DETAIL.

20

WING ROOT UNDERSURFACE

Underplan, Mk I
Port side ▼

ROUNDEL UNDER STARBOARD WING ONLY.

STARBOARD UNDERSURFACE – SKG.

AILERON – B.

THIS WING SHOWS STARBOARD UPPER SURFACE CAMOUFLAGE.

CAMERA WINDOW

BOMBS: DG & WHITE BAND.

STRINGERS OMITTED FROM PLAN VIEW FOR CLARITY.

THIS SIDE OF TAILPLANE SHOWS UPPER CAMOUFLAGE PATTERN.

UNDERSURFACE OF ENTIRE TAILPLANE IS – SKG.

Colour code
DE – Dark Earth; **DG** – Dark Green; **BRO** – Bronze; **B** – Black; **Y** – Yellow; **SKG** – Sky grey; **NM** – Natural metal; **Si** – Silver; **RR** – Roundel Red; **W** – White; **RBL** – Roundel Blue; **SK** – Sky (Duck Egg Blue). Guns – Dark grey; ammunition belts – NM; Vickers gun drums – NM sides, B tops, with leather strap.

Plan view, Mk I ►
Port side

◄ **Scrap plan view, Mk II**
Port tailplane

Numerical key (main drawings)
1. Oil tank. 2. Instrument panel. 3. Chart table. 4. Fuel tank. 5. Gunner's control panel and instruments. 6. Drift sight. 7. Altimeter and air speed indicator (port side). 8. Swivel seat. 9. Vickers 'K' gun. 10. Control column. 11. Camera (port side). 12. Radio (port side). 13. Batteries (port side). 14. Ammunition for spat machine guns. 15. Oil cooler and cockpit heater. 16. Ammunition tanks. 17. Ammunition drums. 18. Aerial winch. 19. Steps. 20. Gun sights (reflector sight fitted later). 21. Seat raising wheel. 22. Four passengers (max).

A Lysander II, its rear canopy slid to reveal the Vickers K gun and mounting. Notice the variation in fin flash design between this aircraft and its squadron stablemate depicted opposite.
▼

Front elevation, Mk I ▶

MARK III.

PITOT HEAD.

REAR STRUT.

'X'

BOMBS ON LIGHT SERIES CARRIERS. PORT SIDE SIMILAR.

MARK III SAS.

SINGLE LIGHT SERIES CARRIER AND SUPPLY CONTAINER. STARBOARD SIDE SIMILAR.

Scrap underplan, Mk I
Full fuselage
▼

MARK III TAILWHEEL.

RACK BRACING STRUTS 'X'.

RACK - MM

B

Scale

0 1 2 3 4 5 6 7 8 ft
0   1   2 m

The fuselage structure laid bare, showing the U-section gusset plates forward and welded steel-tubing construction aft. Wooden stringers, not present here, formed the framework for the fabric covering.
▼

Close up views showing (clockwise from top left) starboard wheel spat and landing light; port wing strut attachment; exhaust pipe detail; and pilot's cockpit glazing, port side. ▶

Sketch section

Key to cockpit and armament sketches

1. Aerial winch (trailing aerial). 2. Barrel lock for machine gun. 3. Spare ammunition containers. 4. Swivelling seat. 5. Chart table (fuel tank below). 6. Radio. 7. Camera. 8. Battery. 9. Pilot's seat pan (natural metal). 10. Fuel pressure (green). 11. Oil pressure (yellow). 12. Boost-manifold pressure (red rim). 13. Ammeter. 14. Rev counter (black rim). 15. Compass lamp switch. 16. Pilot's services switches. 17. Push button for gunner's warning lamp. 18. Morse key. 19. Cowl gills control. 20. Seat raising wheel. 21. TR9 radio control (Mk I only). 22. Side window retracted. 23. Leather padding. 24. Tailplane trimmer control. 25. Radio socket for helmet lead. 26. Engine primer pump. 27. Engine starting panel. 28. Engine priming cock. 29. Engine data plate. 30. Air intake control. 31. Cockpit heating control. 32. Oil warming control. 33. Oil temperature (yellow rim). 34. Carburettor air control. 35. Rudder bar adjustment. 36. Control column (with brake lever and gun button). 37. Propeller pitch control. 38. Throttle lever. 39. Mixture control. 40. VHF radio selector. 41. Landing lamp switch. 42. Fuel cock. 43. Fuel gauge. 44. Oxygen control. 45. Ignition switches. 46. Air pressure gauge. 47. Flare switch. 48. Rear gun sight. 49. Rudder pedals. 50. Mount for reflector sight. 51. Compass. 52. Mounting position for eight Very light cartridges. 53. Bomb selector switches. 54. Bomb release lever and jettison switch. 55. Clock.

MARK I. PANEL.

BOMB RACK DETAIL.

GUN ON UNIVERSAL ROCKING MOUNTING.

MARK I. GUNNER'S COCKPIT.

VICKERS 'K' GUN DETAIL.
SIGHTS.
LEATHER STRAP.
FLASH ELIMINATOR.
AMMUNITION DRUM.
HAND GRIP.
TRIGGER.
EJECTED CARTRIDGE CASE BAG.

MARK III COCKPIT.
(ALL PANELS COLOURED DULL BLACK.)
(COCKPIT INTERIOR IS MATT LIGHT GREEN.)

BLIND FLYING PANEL:- AS MARK III.

BLIND FLYING PANEL KEY.

	LEFT.	CENTRE.	RIGHT.
UPPER ROW.	AIRSPEED INDICATOR.	ARTIFICIAL HORIZON.	CLIMB/DESCENT.
LOWER ROW.	ALTIMETER.	DIRECTION GYRO.	TURN/SLIP.

Scrap views, Mks I and III ▲
Mercury engine

EXHAUST PIPES.

CYL. BAFFLES. SUMP.

SEE FUSELAGE CUT-AWAY VIEW FOR INSTALLATION.

INDUCTION PIPES, (REAR OF CYLINDERS.)

ENGINE COLOUR DATA:-
CYLINDERS AND BAFFLE PLATES: MATT LIGHT GREY.

ALL OTHER PARTS: SEMI-MATT BLACK.

EXHAUST PIPES.

BAFFLES.

INDUCTION PIPES REAR OF CYLINDERS.

CYLINDERS REMOVED FOR CLARITY.

▲
Scrap views, Mk II
Perseus engine

M.A.BARNES 1979

Scrap plan views
Gunner's cockpit
▼

GUNNER'S COCKPIT.

·303" BROWNINGS.
(MARK III A.)

·303" VICKERS 'K' GUN
(MARK I & II.)

GUNS SHOWN ERECT,
IN 'ACTION' POSITION.

TRANSVERSE BAR HERE,
FRONT LEFT TO REAR
RIGHT;(SEE PLAN VIEW.)

SIDE SCREENS LOWERED,
TOP HATCH OPEN.

Scrap inboard profile ▲
Starboard side

Cutaway drawing
By Tony Barnes

Piper J3C Cub

Country of origin: USA.
Type: Two-seat, land-based trainer.
Dimensions: Wing span 35ft 2½in *10.73m*; length 22ft 4½in *6.82m*; height 6ft 8in *2.03m*; wing area 178.5 sq ft *16.58m²*.

Weights: Empty 680lb *308kg*; loaded 1220lb *553kg*.
Powerplant: One Continental, Lycoming or Franklin four-cylinder, horizontally opposed engine rated at 65hp.
Performance: Maximum speed 87mph

140kph; initial climb rate 450ft/min *135m/min*; service ceiling 11,500ft *3500m*; range 206 miles *330km*.
Armament: None.
Service: First flight (J3) late 1937.

Port elevation ▶

Starboard elevation
Wing omitted to show structure
▼

▲
Scrap underplan
Axles, shock absorbers and cabane struts omitted

DRAWN BY MAURICE BRETT

The Cub family represented one of the most popular light aircraft designs of all time, the basic 40hp version originally selling for a mere $995! This is a US Army L-4. (M Brett)
▼

POSITION & SIZE OF EARLY STYLE MARKINGS

TRANSPARENT INSPECTION PANEL

AILERON CABLE IN FAIRLEADS ON REAR OF STRUT

IG-AXHR

◄ **Underplan**
Port side

AERIAL FAIRLEAD

HANDGRIPS

TYPICAL IRREGULAR MEDIUM GREEN BLOTCHES ON LEADING & TRAILING EDGES.

WHITE BARS (INVASION MARKINGS)

BLACK BARS

▲ **Plan view**
Port side

Scale

0 1 2 3 4 5 6 7 8 ft

0   1   2 m

▲ Early-production L-4A, its serial number displayed on a piece of paper stuck inside the rear glazing! Just visible is the generator mounted centrally on the undercarriage struts. (M Brett)

Restored L-4H with D-Day invasion stripes and typical US Army scheme of OD overall with Medium Green patches along leading and trailing edges of flying surfaces.
▼

329 601

ENGINE COOLING AIR SCOOP

JURY STRUTS

OLIVE DRAB ABOVE THIS LINE

NEUTRAL GRAY BELOW

COOLING AIR INTAKE (SOMETIMES BLANKED OFF)

CARBURETTER COLD AIR INTAKE & FILTER

HEATER AIR INTAKE

FOOTREST

HYDRAULIC BRAKE LINES

▲ **Front elevation**

Scrap views
Interior details

Fuselage cross-sections

Labels (upper-left scrap view):
AERIAL FAIRLEAD — AERIAL WINCH — RADIO PANEL — HEADSET — TAIL TRIM WINDER — VERTICAL SLIDING WINDOW PANEL — FUEL COCK CONTROL — THROTTLE LEVER (2) — INSTRUMENTS — FUEL FILLER — FUEL TANK — FUEL COCK — FUEL SUPPLY TO FILTER & ENGINE — FRONT RUDDER PEDAL — FRONT BRAKE PEDAL & LEVER — OPTIONAL GENERATOR — SCOTT TYPE BRAKE CYLINDER — REAR BRAKE PEDAL — CARB. HEAT CONTROL (STBD ONLY) — CONTROL ASSEMBLY MOUNTING BRACKET — AILERON CONTROL CRANK — ELEVATOR CONTROL CRANK — BACK SUPPORT STRAP (FWD. POSITION SHOWN DOTTED) — SEAT BELT CLIPS — PLY FOOTBOARDS — RUDDER CABLE — ELEVATOR CONTROL CABLES — TAIL TRIM CABLES — RADIO — G — G

Labels (lower-left scrap view):
PLY CHART BOARD — RADIO — SEAT PAN — THROTTLE LEVER — REAR BRAKE PEDAL — PLY FLOOR WITH ALUM. KICK PLATES — FRONT BRAKE PEDAL — FRONT RUDDER PEDAL — REAR RUDDER PEDAL — BRAKE OPERATING LEVER — BRAKE CYLINDER — ALUM CONICAL COVER OVER AILERON CABLE — SEAT SUPPORT TUBES — RUDDER CABLE — ELEVATOR CABLES

SECTION ON G-G PART CUT-AWAY TO SHOW FLOOR LEVEL FITTINGS

Labels (A-A section):
EXHAUST MANIFOLD — ENGINE MOUNT — AIR HEATER SHROUD — HEATER AIR INTAKE PIPES — CABIN HEATER & VENTILATOR — EXHAUST PIPE — CARB HEAT SUPPLY — A-A

Labels (B-B section):
COMPASS — A.S.I. — ALTIMETER — CABIN HEAT — OIL TEMP — OIL PRESS — PRIMER — FUEL TANK — REV. COUNTER — FUEL COCK & CONTROL — BRAKE OP. LEVER — CABIN HEATER INLET — FRONT RUDDER PEDAL — BRAKE PEDAL — B-B

Labels (C-C section):
WINGSPAR — FRONT WING ATTACHMENT — THROTTLE LEVERS — TAIL TRIM WINDER — REAR RUDDER PEDAL — BRAKE PEDAL — BRAKE CYLINDER — C-C

Labels (D-D section):
REAR WING ATTACHMENT — FABRIC — AERIAL FAIRLEAD — WINGSPAR — CLIPS FOR CONTROL COLUMN STOWAGE — AERIAL WINCH — OPTIONAL RADIO — HARNESS ATTACHMENT — CHART BOARD SHELF — SEAT PAN — FABRIC COVERING — REAR SEAT SUPPORT — RUDDER CABLE FAIRLEAD — PLY FOOTBOARDS — BACK SUPPORT STRAP — ELEVATOR CONTROL LEVER — D-D

Labels: E-E — F-F

Labels (enlarged view):
SCREW JACK — TAILPLANE YOKE — TAILPLANE L.E. — CABLE TENSIONER & JOCKEY PULLEY — TRIMMER CABLES

ENLARGED VIEW ON TAIL TRIM CONTROL MECHANISM SEE SECTION F-F

Piper O-59 Cub photographed in May 1943. Early civilian Cubs had less extensive glazing, and none at all above the heads of the crew. (Crown Copyright)

Scale

0 1 2 3 4 5 6 7 8 ft

0 1 2 m

Wing cross-sections
▼

PITOT HEAD (PORT ONLY)

JURY STRUTS & SPACER ARRANGEMENT

AIRFOIL SECTION USA 35 B

AILERON SPAR BRACE (BETWEEN RIBS)

CONTROL HORN STOPS

AILERON PIVOT

WING RIB AT AILERON CONTROL HORN SCALE X2
WOODEN SPAR WING WITH FRISE AILERONS

WIRE BRACE

FIN POST

ELEVATOR

2-PIECE CENTRAL ELEVATOR HORN

DISTANCE PIECE

TAILPLANE PIVOT

FUSELAGE UPPER LONGERON

SCREW JACK

TAILPLANE YOKE

TAILPLANE

JOCKEY PULLEY

TRIM CABLES

TAILWHEEL STEERING HORN (OPTIONAL)

RUDDER HORN

ELEVATOR CONTROL CABLE

SCALE X 2

TAILPLANE PIVOT BRACKET

SCRAP VIEW ABOVE OF TAILPLANE AND ELEVATOR CONTROLS

WING ATTACHMENT POINTS

OIL TANK FILLER

¼" CHANNEL SECTION STEEL FAIRING STRUCTURE (EARLIER MODELS USED WOODEN STRIPS)

WELDED STEEL TUBE FRAME

GUIDES FOR SLIDING WINDOW (PORT ONLY)

★ STBD SIDE ONLY DOTTED MEMBERS PORT SIDE ONLY

FAIRING STRUCTURE

OIL TANK

ALL ENGINE DETAILS PAINTED BLACK

CRANKCASE BREATHER

CARBURETTOR INTAKE & FILTER

INSTALLATION OF CONTINENTAL A65

OIL TANK

EXHAUST MANIFOLDS OMITTED ON THESE VIEWS

EXHAUST PIPE

AIR HEATER SHROUD

HEATER AIR INTAKE

CARB HEAT AIR SUPPLY

CABIN HEATER AND VENTILATOR

WIRE BRACING WELDED TO TUBE

ELEVATOR HORN

EXTENT OF ALUM SHEET NOSE CAPPING —
UPPER
LOWER

ASH TIP BOW

INTERNAL AILERON CABLE & PULLEY

EXTERNAL AILERON CABLE & PULLEYS

UNDERSIDE OF PORT WING FRAME WOODEN SPARS FRISE AILERONS

¼" CHANNEL STIFFENERS

▲ **Scrap views**
Fuselage structure and engine details

Macchi C200 Saetta

Country of origin: Italy.
Type: Single-seat, land-based fighter.
Dimensions: Wing span 34ft 8½in
10.58m; length 26ft 10½in *8.20m*; height
11ft 6in *3.51m*; wing area 180.8 sq ft
16.8m².
Weights: Empty 3903lb *1770kg*; loaded

4851lb *2200kg.*
Powerplant: One Fiat A74 RC.38 radial
engine rated at 840hp.
Performance: Maximum speed 303mph
488kph at 15,000ft *4570m*; time to 3280ft
1000m, 1.05min; service ceiling 33,000ft
10,060m; range (normal) 354 miles

570km.
Armament: Two fixed 12.7mm Breda-
SAFAT machine guns, plus (late models)
two fixed 7.7mm machine guns.
Service: First flight (prototype) 24
December 1937; service entry autumn
1939.

▲ Port elevation

▲ Front elevation

The Saetta (Arrow) proved to be an
exceptionally stable, very agile fighter,
though, in comparison with
contemporary German and Allied
types, underarmed. (M Passingham)
▼

▲
The C200's early enclosed canopy was disliked by Italian pilots and eventually discarded in favour of a semi-open cockpit, as here. (M Passingham)

▲
Rear elevation

Scale

0 1 2 3 4 5 6 7 8 ft

0   1   2 m

▲
Fuselage cross-sections

il flaps   a a   b b   c c   d d   e e

heated pitot

ceramic insulator

cooling louvres

oil radiator from soldered brass

Plan view ▼

Underplan
▼

flaps hydr. actuator

W – W

A – A

▲
Wing cross-sections

DEFLECTIONS

±25°	Elevator
±30°	Rudder
±25°	Ailerons
45°	
+1.45° / –5.30°	Stab

Aer. Macchi
C.200
P.V.·Kg 1960
C.U.·Kg 519

M.M.7705

Starboard elevation ▼

C.G.

Late-production Saetta in pristine, factory finish of dark green and light grey, with yellow cowling and white fuselage band. (Pilot Press)
▼

hand hold open

chiusura tettuccio sganciata

armour plate

canopy lock open

cockpit opening & gun sight

canopy pivot

some side controls
omitted for clarity

rudder

floor

ailerons

flaps

Scrap views (not to scale)
Interior details

Scrap views (not to scale) ▶
Fiat A74RC.38 engine

Motor
Fiat
A.74 R.C. 38

strut compr.   max escursione

brake lines

Scrap views (not to scale)
Undercarriage details

Gregor FDB-1

Country of origin: Canada.
Type: Single-seat, land-based fighter/dive-bomber.
Dimensions: Wing span 28ft 0in *8.53m*; length 22ft 0¼in *6.71m*; wing area 194 sq ft *18.02m²*.
Weights: Empty 2280lb *1034kg*; loaded 4100lb *1859kg*.

Powerplant: One Pratt & Whitney R-1535-SB4-G Twin Wasp Junior fourteen-cylinder radial engine rated at 750hp.
Performance: Maximum speed 261mph *420kph*; initial climb rate 2800ft/min *850m/min*; absolute ceiling 27,700ft

8440m; range (clean) about 1000 miles *1600km*.
Armament: Provision for two fixed 0.50in machine guns, plus two 116lb *53kg* bombs.
Service: First flight 3 March 1939.

▲ **Scrap view (1/24th scale)**
Fin legend

▲ **Port elevation**

Fuselage cross-sections
▼

▲ **Scrap port elevation**
Showing interior detail

Designed by Russian emigré Michael Gregor, the FDB-1 was rolled out in December 1938 for a series of publicity photos at Fort William, Ontario. Guns would have been installed in the upper wing centre section. (H Robinson)
▼

Front elevation
▼

Scrap views (1/48th scale)
Propeller details
▼

EARLY SPINNER (2)

FINAL SPINNER (3)

CRANK-CASE SKIRT (3)   L.E. COWLINGS

Scrap views (1/48th scale)
Undercarriage details
▼

DETAILS OF CHAIN & MOTOR DRIVE
TO SPROCKET-GEAR ARE UNKNOWN

ITEMS MARKED Ω
ARE APPROXIMATE

FUSELAGE WITHOUT WELL

WELL WITHOUT CUT-OUT

FULLY
RETRACTED

TENSION SPRING &
CRANK (DOWNLOCK)

SPROCKET-GEAR
ROTATES UPPER
OLEO LEG

NOTE OFF-
SET PIVOT

END OF OLEO LEG
THREE TIMES GIVEN
SCALE

TEMPORARY
RADIUS-RODS (1)

HINGE

FULLY EXTENDED (NO LOAD)   AT ROLLING RADIUS   FULLY EXTENDED

LANDING GEAR RETRACTION.   ONE & A HALF TIMES GIVEN SCALE: TRUE VIEW FROM FRONT.

APPROXIMATE
PIVOT AXIS

FLEXIBLE
FAIRING

COVER DOORS (OMITTED FROM SIDE VIEW)
CURVED SECTION HINGED & SPRING-
MOUNTED ON RADIUS RODS FOR CLOSE
FIT WHEN GEAR RETRACTED.
DETAILS ARE UNKNOWN

FRONT VIEW

GROUNDED DEFLECTION

TAILWHEEL: ONE & A HALF TIMES GIVEN SCALE
DETAILS OF CASTORING ARE UNKNOWN

FDB-1 versions
1. **Original (17/12/38 – Fort William):** Temporary landing gear radius rods; external position lights; no spinner or fin legend.
2. **Intermediate:** Small-diameter spinner, true radius rods.
3. **Final:** Large-diameter spinner with crankcase skirt; black backs to propeller blades (38in long); inset LE position lights; aileron horns and hinges; fin legend.
Note: Numbers shown in parentheses against details refer to these versions. Hole forward of tailplane (both sides) did not appear in final version (3).

The FDB-1, constructed by the Canadian Car & Foundry Co, was probably the last biplane fighter to be built, but it failed to arouse official interest. (H Robinson)
▼

Plan view
▼

OVAL RECESSES IN CENTRE-SECTION ARE THOUGHT TO ENCLOSE AIR EXITS FROM OIL COOLERS & FUEL TANK FILLER CAPS

CANOPY FRAME — RAIL ON FUSELAGE

FIXINGS IN CANOPY FRAME SUGGEST PIVOTING RUNNER AT EACH END TO SUIT CURVE IN RUNNER
CANOPY FRAME & FUSELAGE RAIL
TYPICAL SECTION: SIX TIMES GIVEN SCALE

Colour notes
Overall finish – deep gunmetal blue ('a little lighter than a rifle barrel'); registration lettering – aluminium; propeller/spinner, wheels and landing gear members and interior of cover doors – natural metal; early landing gear radius rods – believed light grey (1); 'CCF Co' legend on fin – white; rudder striping – red/white.

Scrap views (not to scale) ▼
Aileron controls

AILERON CONTROLS ARE APPROXIMATE

OUTBOARD

INBOARD
AILERON HINGES

Scale
0 1 2 3 4 5 6 7 8 ft
0 1 2 m

COWL PANELS ARE SCREW-FASTENED

Scrap views (1/36th scale) ▶
Air speed pitot tubes

AILERON HORN

EXTERNAL HINGES & CONTROL HORN TO AILERON NOT FITTED UNTIL FINAL VERSION (3)

FABRIC-COVERED AILERON

METAL-COVERED FLAPS (UPPER & LOWER WINGS)

FRONT
SIDE
VIEW & DETAILS AT LEFT SHOW ORIGINAL (1) & (2)
WING-TIP POSITION LIGHTS
METAL SURROUNDS ARE UNPAINTED

▲
Underplan

◀ **Scrap underplan**
Starboard upper wing

Typical upper wing cross-section
▼

HANDLEY-PAGE AUTOMATIC SLOT

DURAL SEMI-BOX SPARS: CHANNEL FLANGES WITH SINGLE STEPPED WEB
DURAL COVERING
FLAP
AILERON

TWICE GIVEN SCALE

DRAWN BY HARRY ROBINSON

▲
Scrap plan view
Starboard lower wing

Douglas SBD-3 and -5 Dauntless

Country of origin: USA.
Type: Two-seat, carrier-based scout/dive bomber.
Dimensions: Wing span 41ft 0in *12.50m*; length 32ft 0in *9.75m*; height 13ft 0in *3.96m*; wing area 325 sq ft *30.19m²*.
Weights: Empty 6535lb *2964kg*; loaded 9519lb *4317kg*.
Powerplant: One Wright R-1820-52

Cyclone nine-cylinder radial engine rated 1000hp, (-5) R-1820-60 rated at 1200hp.
Performance: Maximum speed 255mph *411kph* at 14,000ft *4265m*; time to 10,000ft *3050m*, 7min; service ceiling 25,200ft *7680m*; range (max bomb load) 450 miles *725km*.
Armament: One 1000lb *454kg* or 500lb

227kg bomb on fuselage cradle and two 100lb *45kg* bombs on wing racks, plus two fixed 0.5in Browning and one or (-5) two flexibly mounted 0.3in machine guns.
Service: First flight (XBT-1) July 1935; service entry (SBD-1) 4 June 1940, (-3) December 1940.

▲ Port elevation, SBD-5

▲ Fuselage cross-sections

▼ Scrap port elevation, SBD-3

▲ Starboard elevation, SBD-5

Scale

LETTERBOX SLOTS

ACCESS PANELS

BOMB RACK

BOMB YOKE

INSIDE WHEEL WELLS ZC

LANDING LAMP

PITOT

FABRIC COVERED AILERON

INSIDE OF DIVE - BRAKES RO

▲
Underplan, SBD-5

A number of SBD-5s were supplied to the French Navy postwar, seeing action in Indo-China. (ECA) ▼

FABRIC COVERED ELEVATOR

TAILWHEEL SOLID ON SBD PNEUMATIC ON A-24

▲
Dauntless in civilian hands in the 1950s,
apparently fitted for skywriting. Other
ex-military SBDs were used for crop-
dusting. (J Gradidge)

Plan view, SBD-5
▼

FLANGE FAIRING

LETTERBOX SLOTS

FORMATION LIG

TRIM TAB – PORT ONLY

RUNNING LIGHT

PERFORATED DIVE–BRAKE

AILERON CONSTRUCTION

WING WALK M8

* STENCIL ON HATCH:
LIFE RAFT &
EMERGENCY
RATIONS

Scale
0 1 2 3 4 5 6 7 8 ft
0   1   2 m

▲
Wing cross-sections

TRIM TAB

ELEVATOR CONSTRUCTION

Front elevation, SBD-5 ▼

OFFSET MAST

BULLETPROOF GLASS

UC PIVOT

PITOT

MEAN DIHEDRAL ANGLE: 10°

RACK FOR 100 LB BOMB

UC RETRACTION 96°

NM

WHEELS 30 X 7

FLAP/DIVE-BRAKE CONFIGURATION (NOT TO SCALE)

LANDING POSITION

DIVING POSITON

SBD-5 DIVED AT 70°, 276 M.P.H.

FREISE-TYPE AILERON DETAIL
(NOT TO SCALE)

◄ **Scrap views (not to scale)**
Flap/dive brake configuration

O

MB

MAKER'S BADGE

HAMILTON STANDARD HYDROMATIC AIRSCREW
DIAMETER 10'9"

▲
Propeller details

Colour code
LSB – Light smoky blue; **VPG** – Very pale grey;
RB – Dirty royal blue; **ZC** – ZC (zinc chromate)
green; **R** – Red; **W** – White; **O** – Orange; **RO** –
Red-orange; **PY** – Pale yellow; **MB** – Matt
black; **IB** – Insignia Blue (Navy); **NM** – Natural
metal.

R
W
IB
RB

① UNTIL 17.8.42

② 18.8.42 – 29.6.43

③

30.6.43 – SEPT. 43

④

SEPT. 43 ON

▲
Scrap views (not to scale)
National insignia

**Summary of external differences,
SBD-5 and SBD-3**
1. Air intake on cowl top, SBD-3; absent on
SBD-5.
2. Three cowl gills, SBD-3; one on SBD-5.
3. External gunsight, SBD-3; absent on
SBD-5.
4. Single gun in rear cockpit, SBD-3; twin
guns in SBD-5.

DRAWN BY D PLATT

Focke-Wulf Fw 190A-5, A-9, F and G

Country of origin: Germany.
Type: Single-seat, land-based fighter and (F, G) fighter-bomber.
Dimensions: Wing span 34ft 5½in *10.5m*; length 29ft 0in *8.84m*; height 13ft 0in *3.96m*; wing area 196.98 sq ft *18.3m²*.
Weights: Empty 7000lb *3176kg*, (F) 7328lb *3325kg*; normal loaded 9750lb *4424kg*, (F) 9700lb *4401kg*; maximum 10,800lb *4900kg*, (F) 10,850lb *4923kg*.
Powerplant: One BMW 801D fourteen-cylinder radial engine rated at 1700hp,

(A-9) 801F rated at 2000hp, (F, G) 801D-2 rated at 1700hp.
Performance: Maximum speed (clean) 408mph *657kph* at 20,670ft *6300m*, (F, clean) 394mph *634kph* at 18,050ft *5500m*; initial climb rate 2350ft/min *720m/min*, (F) 2110ft/min *640m/min*; service ceiling 33,800ft *10,300m*, (F) 34,800ft *10,600m*; range (normal) 500 miles *800km*.
Armament: Two fixed 20mm MG 151 cannon, two fixed 20mm MG FF cannon and two fixed 7.9mm MG 17 machine

guns, (A-9) four fixed 20mm MG 151 cannon and two fixed 13mm MG 131 machine guns, (F) two fixed 20mm MG 151 cannon and two fixed 7.9mm MG 17 machine guns plus one 550lb *250kg* bomb, (G) two fixed 20mm MG 151 cannon plus one 1100lb *500kg*, 2200 *1000kg* or 3960lb *1800kg* bomb.
Service: First flight (Fw 190V-1) 1 June 1939, (F) late 1942; service entry (A-5) summer 1943, (G) autumn 1943.

Starboard elevation, Fw 190F-2

Blown hood shown below was introduced on the FW 190F-2, although was not used on this particular aircraft

FW 190F-2 of Gefechtsverband Druschel on the Eastern front showing the tropical air filters commonly used by aircraft in this theater

Fin, rudder, and fuselage sides 76 mottled 02

Firescreen upper flame destroyer and 'Coalbox' lower flame destroyer

Exhaust deflector plates

SD 500 Bomb

ER 4 Bomb carrier with 4 x SC 50 bombs

AB 500 Bomb dispenser

AB 250 Bomb dispenser

▲ **Scrap starboard elevation, Fw 190A-5/U2**
Wk Nr 1083, Ge+LA

FW 190A-5, This view also serves:-
FW 190F-2, less outer wing guns
FW 190G-2, less outer wing guns and fuselage guns
Position of FuG 216 radar aerials on
FW 190A-6/R 11 night fighters

Exhaust flame shield used on night intruders and night fighters

ETC 501 Rack
SC 500 Bomb
Radar aerials on FW 190A-6/R11 night fighters, stbd wing root only
SC 250 Bomb

SB 1000 Bomb lower fin omitted to provide ground clearence

LTF 5b Torpedo carried on an ETC 502 rack on the FW 190A-5/U14

▲ **Port elevation, Fw 190A-5**

Scale

0 1 2 3 4 5 6 7 8ft

0 1 2m

Spinner B
spiral W

75   74   75

70

This view also serves:—
FW 190F-3, less outer wing guns
        plus ETC 501 rack
FW 190G-3, less outer wing guns
        and fuselage guns,
        plus ETC 501 rack

Rüstsatz 6 (R6)
WGr 21 Rocket launcher.
A-5, A-6, A-7, A-8.

WGr 28/32 successor to the WGr 21,
shown here in the twin launcher.
F-8

B
B   Z.70004
W

Fin and rudder 76
mottled with 82

Tail unit showing
lengthened tail
wheel leg on
FW 190A-5/U14

WBY   74 ⓐ ⓑ

ⓒ

R

ⓔ 76 ⓓ

B W
Y

▲
Port elevation, Fw 190A-6
1/JG54 (believed flown by Walter Novotney)

Port elevation, Fw 190A-7/R6
JG1, Oesau, Germany, 1943
▼

Spinner HG 65
spiral R

75   74

70

R ①

Lower cowling
doors only

①

The R6 installation has been omitted from
this view for clarity.

WRWR   BWB 74 WR 75

ⓜ

B   317822

Rudder
R

ⓐ   ⓑ
ⓒ

ⓓ

Fin, rudder, and fuselage
sides 76 lightly mottled
with 74

**Fw 190 prototype, probably the V5, the first to be powered
by the BMW 801 engine. (J Brindley)**
▼

Scale

FW 190 A-6 of 6/JG.26
Germany, March 1944

Fin, rudder and fuselage
sides 76 lightly mottled
with 02

Starboard elevation, Fw 190A-6 ▶
6/JG26, Germany, March 1944

Rüstsatz 1 (R1)
4 x MG 151 paired
in gun packs
under each wing.
A-6, A-7, A-8, A-9,
F-3, F-8, G-3.

Experimental installation of
RB Mk 108 in underwing
fairings

Rüstsatz 3 (R3) RB Mk 103
in underwing fairings. Late
production style top, early
production style bottom.
A-6, A-7, A-8, A-9,
F-3, F-8, F-9.

Rear fairing frequently
removed in front line
service

Starboard elevation, Fw 190A-8/R8
Flown by Unteroffizier Maximowitz,
IV/JG3, summer 1944
▼

MG 131's removed from
this particular aircraft

Fin, rudder, fuselage sides 76
mottled with 02

External armour plate

ETC 501 rack on this
aircraft set up to
carry bombs

ETC 504 torpedo rack on
FW 190F-8/U14 did away
with the need for the
lengthened tail wheel leg ↓

Spinner R
spiral Y

Tail unit fitted to
FW 190F-8/U3 showing
lengthened tail wheel in
the retracted position and
rudder moved further aft

Broad chord wooden
propellers were
fitted to a few late
production aircraft

Scrap starboard elevation, Fw 190F-8/U3 ▶
Showing revised bomb rack

LT 950

BT 1400

Lower fin folded to increase
ground clearance

FW 190F-8/U3 with
revised bomb rack

The view below serves for
FW 190A-8 & A-9
FW 190F-8 & F-9, less outer wing guns
FW 190G-8, less outer wing guns and
fuselage mounted guns

Spinner B
spiral W

Fin, rudder, fuselage
sides 76

Maximum compression
Static ground line
Maximum extension

Position of ETC 501 rack and rear fairings
hinged down to allow access doors to
wing root MG 151 ammunition boxes to be
opened for reloading

▲
Port elevation, Fw 190A-8
Volkel, Holland, autumn 1944

DRAWN BY A L BENTLEY

An early-production 190 up on trials, 7 September 1942. Within six months, the Focke-Wulf Fw 190 would account for almost half of Germany's fighter production. (J Brindley)

Other aircraft served by this view:—
FW 190A-7 & A-9
FW 190F-7 as for A-7 less outer wing guns
FW 190F-8 as for A-8 less outer wing guns
FW 190F-9 as for A-9 less outer wing guns
FW 190G-8 as for A-8 less outer wing guns and fuselage mounted guns

MG 151 20mm cannon was the standard outer wing gun for A-7, A-8, and A-9

U/C indicator rod

Camera gun, A-6, A-7, A-8, A-9,

Outboard camera A-5, F-8, G-8.

75 — W Simplified national markings used in the later part of the war

'Doppelreiter' slipper tank position

Position of SG 113A,77mm, downward firing, anti-tank gun, tested on F-8's

This plan view shows the FW 190A-8/R2 showing the fairings over the outer wing gun positions to allow the RB Mk.100 cannon to be fitted inside the wing by the Rüstsatz 2 as an alternative to the standard MG 151 cannons.

Blisters over cannon bays could be seen on F-8 and F-9 machines even though outer wing guns were not normally fitted to these sub types.

Blown canopy introduced on the FW 190F-2 but not widely used until the introduction of the FW 190F-8

Armoured canopy fitted to the FW 190A-8/R7 and FW 190A-8/R8

▲ **Scrap views**
Canopy details

▲ **Plan view, Fw 190A-8/R2**

Colour code

02 – *RLM Grau* (light slate grey); 63 – *Hellblau 65* (light blue); 66 – *Schwarzgrau 66* (black-grey); 70 – *Schwarzgrün 70* (black-green); 71 – *Dunkelgrün 71* (dark green); 74 – *Dunkelgrau 74* (dark grey); 75 – *Mittelgrau 75* (medium grey); 76 – *Hellgrau 76* (light grey); 77 – *Mittelgrau 77* (medium grey); 78 – *Blau 78* (blue); 79 – *Gelb 79* (tan); 80 – *Dunkelgrün 80* (dark green); 81 – *Braunviolett* (brown-violet*); 82 – *Dunkelgrün 82* (dark green*); 83 – *Hellgrün 83* (light green*); W – *Weiss 21* (white**); B – *Schwarz 22* (black**); R – *Rot 23* (red**); BL – *Blau 24* (blue**); G – *Grün 25* (green**); Y – *Gelb 27* (yellow**).

*Replacement colours for 74 and 75.
**Individual aircraft markings colours.

SG 113A installation

Section through Doppelreiter slipper tank tested on FW 190A-8 Works No. 380394 coded 7+

Shown below are the racks for the Panzerblitz 1 (Pb 1) 78 mm modified army rocket projectile and its successor the Panzerblitz 2 (Pb 2) a modified R4M air to air rocket used by FW 190F-9's on the eastern front for tank busting

R4M showing fins folded and deployed (Pb 2)

Panzerblitz 1 (Pb 1)

▲
Scrap views
Armament details

Alternative style of rain guttering to keep camera windows clean

Camera windows

SG 116 upwards firing weapons system tested on a FW 190A-8

(a) (25mm lettering, B)
Hier aufbocken

(b) (20mm lettering, B)
— Anzeigegerät 0

(c) (20mm lettering, W)
Nicht verstellen

(d) (25mm lettering, B)
Reifendruck 5 atü

(e) (25mm lettering, B)
Hier aufbocken

(f) W
R

(g) Y 100mm
B — 200 ltr

(h) W
Y 100mm
B — 232 ltr

(j)

(k) (5mm lettering, W)
Sauerstoff

(i) (25mm lettering, B) Stbd leg
Federbein Solldruck
70 64 54 48 40 35 32 über 4600 kg
58 53 44 38 34 30 27 bis 4600 kg

Port leg
Federbein Solldruck
über 4600kg 32 35 40 48 54 64 70
bis 4600kg 27 30 34 38 44 53 58

Alternatives:- Stbd leg
(20mm & 10mm lettering, B)
Federbeindruck

Port leg
(20mm & 10mm lettering, B)
Federbeindruck

(m) W
Y 100 mm
B

(n) (20mm lettering, B)
Haube
Auf Zu
drücken

(o) (25mm lettering, B)
Reifendruck 5,5 atü

(p) (25mm lettering, W)
Gepäckraum

(q) (25mm lettering, B)
Hier aufbocken

(r) (75mm lettering, 77)
Nur hier betreten

(s) Outline of walkway area
10mm 77 20mm
20mm 20mm

(t) (25mm lettering, W)
ACHTUNG !

(u) (15mm lettering, W)
Haubenabwurf durch Sprengladung

▲
Stencilled instructions
See main drawings for location

Fw 190As stand ready at a Channel coast airfield. The unit appears to be either *JG2* or *JG26*. (J Brindley)
▼

Scale

0 1 2 3 4 5 6 7 8 ft

0   1   2m

Early style upper
wing surface cross

◄ **Plan view, Fw 190A-5**

FuG 216 radar aerials on
FW 190A-6/R11 night fighters

FuG 216 radar aerials
on FW 190A-6/R11
night fighters

Plan view of FW 190-5. The canopy is shown
open, clearly showing the canopy rails not being
parallel. To enable the canopy to slide and the
runners to stay in the rails, a hinge is fitted
into the top of the canopy to allow the front
of the canopy to bend to follow the rails.
This plan view also serves for the FW 190A-6
by the introduction of the MG 151 cannons in
the outer wing gun position

FuG 216 radar
aerials on
FW 190A-6/R11
night fighters

MG 151
FW 190A-6

Other aircraft served by this view:-
FW190F-2 as for A-5 less outer wing guns
FW190F-3 as for A-6 less outer wing guns
FW190G-2 as for A-5 less outer wing guns
        and engine mounted guns
FW190G-3 as for A-6 less outer wing guns
        and engine mounted guns

FuG 216 radar aerials on
FW 190A-6/R11 night
fighters

Port elevation, Fw 190S-5 ▼
Wing omitted to show detail

The camouflage pattern on this aircraft extended
down the fuselage sides forward of the markings
to the top surface of the wings.

FW 190S-5 with wing removed to show
details of the wing root fairings Armament
was not normally fitted to two seat aircraft

75 (83?)

Tailplane pivot
bracket

Rear spar pick up point

FW 190S-8, Altenburg, September 1944. Wing and tailplane
removed to show details of the lower fuselage sides, wing
pick up points; and tailplane pivot bracket. Also shown is
the revised rear canopy side windows to improve forward
view for the instructor

Front spar pick up points
Fuselage datum
Wing datum

▲
Starboard elevation, Fw 190S-8
Altenburg, September 1944

Fuselage datum
Wing datum

Rudder hinge datum
Elevator hinge datum

Propeller datum

Wing pick up points

Tailplane pivot bracket

Top view of improved rear cockpit canopy

Scrap views
Armament details
▼ ▶

Rüstsatz 1 (R1) 2 x MG 151

Link chute

Port outer wing gun bay door for MG151 20mm cannon fitted to aircraft with enlarged openings to gun bay

▲
Scrap plan view, Fw 190S-5
Armament not normally fitted to two-seat aircraft

Pitot used with alternative radar aerials for FW 190A-6/R11 night fighters

Radar aerials on FW 190A-6/R11 night fighters, stbd wing root only

FW 190A-6/R11 night fighters had an ETC 501 rack for a 300 litre tank, and inner wheel doors removed and replaced with the fixed fairings

Holes for attachment screws for rear part of fairing for ETC 501

Underplan, Fw 190F-8, G-8
Port wing and fuselage rack
▼

Step

Standard undersurface colours :-
European and Eastern front 76
Tropical (Mediterranean) area) 78

Inner wheel doors fitted to most FW 190A-6 aircraft

ETC 71
ETC 50

Underplan, Fw 190A-6 ▶

FW 190A-6 showing the wing with revised internal structure and MG 151's in outer wing gun bays

Alternative radar aerials for FW190A-6/R11 night fighters

Inboard camera gun installation

Rüstsatz 1 (R1) Sealing panel to outer wing gun bay shows enlarged hatch for R2 installation

Scrap views
Main undercarriage details
▼

Detail of main undercarriage leg

0° 10' 4"

Pintle axis
Motor axis

7° 50' 11"

15° 0' 10"

36° 0' 0"

Motor axis   Pintle axis

Wing datum

700mm x 175mm

Sliding lower U/C leg door frequently left off in front line service on fighter bombers

Pick up points for R6 support tubes and Messerschmitt racks

ETC 501 rack
Focke Wulf rack
Rüstsatz 3 (R3)
Pick up points for R6 support tubes and Messerschmitt racks

Underplan, Fw 190A-5, F-2, G-2 ▶
Starboard wing

Front bomb support arms retracted

ETC 50 Bomb racks F-3, F-8, G-8.

ETC 71 Bomb racks, F-8, F-9.

Panzerblitz 1 (PB1) rocket launching rails, F-8

Panzerblitz 2 (PB2) rocket launching rails, F-8.

Early camera gun installation

Leading edge of FW190A-5/U2 night intruder showing landing lights and outboard mounting for camera gun

Tropical air filters A-5, F-2, F-3, F-8, G-2, G-8.

Underplan, Fw 190A-5/Trop ▼

Underneath view of FW190A-5/Tp showing the ETC 501 rack fitted with mounting bars for the 300 litre tank, tropical air filters, and the MG FF 20mm cannon installation in the outer wing gun position

Focke Wulf and Weserflug racks for 300 litre long range tanks, A-5

Messerschmitt racks for 300 litre long range tanks, A-5, F-2, F-3, F-8, G-2, G-8.

Rüstsatz 6 (R6) A-5, A-6, A-7, A-8.

Spent shell case chute for RB Mk 108 30mm cannon —blanked off when fitted with MG 151 cannon

Lower fuselage access door introduced on the FW190A-7 series

Experimental installation of RB Mk 108 30mm cannon in underwing fairings

Spent shell case chute

▲ **Underplan, Fw 190A-8/R2**
Showing Rüstsätz 2 installation of RB MK 108 cannon in outer wing gun bay, with enlarged access doors

Flash suppressor horizontal on early installations

Rüstsatz 3 (R3) – early installation

Spent shell case chute

Link chute

Flash suppressor vertical and gun barrel faired in on final installation

Rüstsatz 3 (R3) Late installation with rear fairing shown removed

Spent shell case chute

Link chute

Starboard outer wing gun bay for MG 151 20mm cannon fitted to aircraft with enlarged opening to gun bay

Link chute

ETC 501 wing rack shown with mounting bars for 300 litre long range tanks, A-5,G-3,G-8.

ETC 501 wing rack shown to carry SC 250 kg bomb A-5, G-3, G-8.

▲ **Scrap views** *Armament details*

Scale
0 1 2 3 4 5 6 7 8 ft
0 1 2 m

SC 50 Bombs on ETC 50 racks

Note:- upper bomb fins are semi recessed in rear fairing of the bomb rack

Front elevation, Fw 190A-8/R2
▼

SC 50 Bombs on ETC 71 racks

Panzerblitz 1 (PB 1)

FuG 16ZY aerial

Panzerblitz 2 (PB 2)

Front view of FW190A-8/R2
This view also serves
FW 190A-7 less FuG 16ZY aerial
FW 190A-9
FW 190F-8 & F-9 less outer wing guns
FW 190G-8 less outer wing guns and engine mounted guns

Scrap front elevations
Propeller details
▼

Standard VDM metal propeller. 3300 mm diameter

Wooden propeller seen on a few A-9 and F-9 aircraft in the closing weeks of the war. 3300 mm diameter

▲
Captured G-3 160016 (DN+FP) at Wright Field, USA, in 1943.
(J Brindley)

Experimental installation of RB Mk 100 in underwing fairings

Rüstsatz 1 (R1)

Rüstsatz 3 (R3)
Initial installation

Final installation

Focke Wulf and Weserflug wing racks for 300 litre tanks

Position of tropical air filters

Rüstsatz 6 (R6)

Messerschmitt wing racks for 300 litre tanks

This view also serves
FW 190F-2 & F-3
less outer wing guns
FW 190G-2 & G-3
less outer wing guns
and fuselage guns

300 litre tanks on ETC 501 wing racks

SC 250 bomb on ETC 501 wing racks

Rear view below of FW 190A-5/U8 shown with wing racks removed. This view also serves
FW 190F-2 & F-3
FW 190G-2 & G-3

Front elevation, Fw 190A-5/R6 ▲

Rear elevation, Fw 190A-5/U8 ▼

14 blade cooling fan seen on a few aircraft in the closing weeks of the war

Outboard camera A-5, F-8, G-8.

Outboard camera and landing lights FW 190A-5/U2 Night intruders

Early outboard camera, A-5

Front elevation, Fw 190A-6 ▲

Rear view of FW 190A-5/U4 reconnaissance fighters

Rear view of FW 190S-5 and FW 190S-8 two seat trainers

Rear view of FW 190A-5/U2 night intruders

SG 113A

Doppelreiter slipper tank

Rear view of FW 190A-8/R2 This view also serves for FW 190A-7, 9; FW 190F-8 & F-9 and FW 190G-8 less outer wing guns

Rear elevation, Fw 190A-8/R2 ▲

Cockpit interior details of Fw 190s undergoing postwar restoration, with (lower right) view showing starboard wheel well.
▼

▲
**Fw 190A-4 GL+MY with underbelly rack
and, typically, mottled paintwork on
fuselage sides and denser colouring on
upper surfaces. (RAF Museum)**

Position of FuG 216 radar aerials
on FW 190A-6/R11 night fighters
Alternative type of
radar aerials

▲
Rear elevation, Fw 190A-6

Scale

0 1 2 3 4 5 6 7 8 ft

0 1 2 m

ETC 501 Rack

LTF 5b

ETC 504
Rack

ETC 502
Rack

BT 200
BT 400
BT 700 (or LT 950)
BT 1400

LT 950

Detail of different styles
of 300 litre tanks. The
lower tank was only seen
on aircraft in the closing
weeks of the war

Flattened lower surface

Scrap view
Undercarriage details
▼

Details of inner surfaces
of main U/C doors

Inner face   Outer face
700mm x 175mm main wheel

300mm x 150mm
Tail wheel

Inner wheel door
actuating strut

350mm x 135mm
Tail wheel (A-5,
A-6 intercepters)

BT 200

BT 400

BT 700

▲
Scrap views
Armament details

X-4 wire guided missile tested on F-8's

The two views below show internal details which are typical for
FW 190A-5, A-6, F-2, & F-3. FW 190B-2 & G-2 are similar but
do not carry the MG 17 fuselage guns. FW 190A-7 is also similar
but the MG 17 fuselage guns were replaced by MG 131 guns

Scale

0 1 2 3 4 5 6 7 8 ft
0   1   2 m

MG 17

Inboard profile and plan view
See note for explanation
▼

▲
Inboard profile and plan view
See note for explanation

These two views show internal details which are typical for
FW 190A-8, A-9, F-8, F-9. FW 190G-8 is similar but was
not fitted with MG 131's

MG 131

Fuselage cross-sections
▼

MG 17
MG 131

MG 17
MG 131

Inner U/C door   Fixed fairing

MG 131   MG 17

Main instrument panel

Blown hood

Rüstsätze 3 (R3)
RB.Mk.103

Experimental installation
of RB Mk.108

Rüstsätze 2 (R2)
RB Mk.108

MG FF installion

Wing datum

Rüstsätze 1 (R1)

Wing datum

W.C.D.

Incidence 0°
Theoretical tip section   W.C.D.

Wing datum

Details of
radar aerials

Stbd wing
Port wing

17°
17°   W.C.D.

10°   W.C.D.
60°   Incidence 3°
Wing datum

10°43'35"

30°
25°   4°
           4°

16°
16°

Wing datum
W.C.D.

W.C.D.

W.C.D.

W.C.D.

6°12'10"

Horizontal datum

Wing constructional datum

▲ Wing cross-sections and scrap plan views
Showing armament installations

Scrap views
Main undercarriage details
▼

View on arrow A   14°20'15"

U/C actuating strut   8°56'29"

Scissors link

U/C leg above this line lies
in the plane of the pivot
axis, and below the line in
the plane of the wheel

8°24'22"

View on arrow B

FOCKE WULF FW 190A-5

Drawn by A L Bentley

All dimensions shown have been obtained from offical
Focke Wulf drawings, reports, specifications and data sheets

All dimensions are in millimetres (mm)

General arrangement, Fw 190A-5 to A-9, F and G
1/48th scale (all dimensions in mm)

Inboard views, Fw 190A-8
1/48th scale

RÜSTSÄTZE R.I.

RÜSTSÄTZE R.6.

R.I.

RÜSTSÄTZE R.2.

R.6.

R.2.

Inboard views, Fw 190A-8
1/48th scale

All rib station dimensions outside the main wing box shown immediately below are given in the wing constructional datum plane

All dimensions shown have been obtained from official Focke Wulf drawings, reports, specifications and data sheets

All dimensions are in millimetres (mm)

Scale

Scrap views ▲ ▶
Corrections to night fighter and two-seat variants (note inboard location of aerials)

680
Flap hinge datum
Rear spar datum
Aileron hinge datum
Flap motor
613
MG 151
MG 151

Extra cut-out in late production
A-8,9, & F-8,9, aircraft to
allow Rüstsatz R2 (30mm
RB Mk.108 Cannon in
outer wing)to be fitted

Chord 1200 NACA 23009 Incidence 0°

Wing datum line
25% Chord line, Sweepback 2°30'0"
Front spar datum

Gun alignment
sighting tube
Gun camera

0°8'0"   Toe out 1°30'0"   0°20'24"

MG 17
MG 131
830
680
10,506

Gun alignment
sighting tube   Gun camera   MG FF
MG 151 / RB Mk.108 (R2)

300 MG 151 275 250   210 383 345

MG 151   MG FF
MG 151 (R1)

2415.4
All outer wing guns

930
1220
1400
2370 (MG FF 20mm Cannon)
2375 (MG 151 20mm Cannon and RB Mk.108 30mm Cannon)
2378 (MG 151 20mm Cannon R1. Gondola)
2740 (MG 151 20mm Cannon R1. Gondola)

**General arrangement, Fw 190A-5 to A-9,
F and G**
1/48th scale (all dimensions in mm)

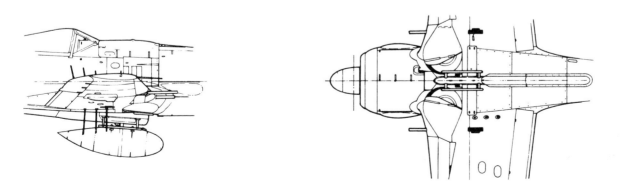

Martin-Baker MB5

Country of origin: Great Britain.
Type: Prototype single-seat, land-based interceptor fighter.
Dimensions: Wing span 35ft 0in *10.67m*; length 37ft 9in *11.51m*; height 15ft 0in *4.57m*; wing area 262.64 sq ft *24.39m²*.
Weights: Empty 9233lb *4189kg*; normal loaded 11,000lb *4991kg*; maximum 12,090lb *5484kg*.
Powerplant: One Rolls-Royce Griffon 83 twelve-cylinder, liquid-cooled piston engine rated at 2340hp.
Performance: Maximum speed 460mph *740kph* at 20,000ft *6095m*; initial climb rate 3800ft/min *1160m/min*; service ceiling 40,000ft *12,190m*; range 1100 miles *1770km*.
Armament: Four fixed 20mm Hispano cannon.
Service: First flight 23 May 1944.

▲ **Port elevation**

DRAWN BY G A HATTON

Colour code
DG – Dark Green; **DSG** – Dark Sea Grey; **MSG** – Medium Sea Grey; **MB** – Matt black; **MY** – Matt yellow.

Regarded by many as the ultimate in piston-engined fighter design, the MB5 was not flown until 1944 and was never to achieve production status.

▼

▲ **Front elevation**

The aggressive, purposeful lines of the MB5 are nicely captured in this photo. Note that the camouflage wraps around the wing leading edge.

Wing cross-section
▼

D

Wing & Fuselage undersides
MSG

Rolls-Royce Griffon 83.

◄ **Plan view**
Starboard side

Scale
0 1 2 3 4 5 6 7 8 ft
0   1   2 m

DG
DSG
DG

D

Wing section – RAF 34.

DG

DG
Fabric
covered
elevators

This tab on
starboard
only.

MSG
DSG

This tab on
port only

DG

Tail undersides
camouflaged

◄ **Propeller details**

MB

MSG

Colour line

DG

DSG

Wheel covers
not fitted

DSG

Split flaps

DSG

DG

Colours shown this side
of centre line are for top
surface, port side only.

Pitot head.

Underplan ▲
Starboard side

Fuselage cross-sections ►   A

B   C

AIRCRAFT ARCHIVE
INDEX TO THE SERIES